Debbie Shore's
SEWING ROOM SECRETS
Machine Sewing

First published in 2019

Search Press Limited
Wellwood, North Farm Road,
Tunbridge Wells, Kent TN2 3DR

Reprinted 2021 (third), 2022 (twice)

Photographs by Garie Hind

ISBN: 978-1-78221-336-9

Suppliers
For details of suppliers, please visit
the Search Press website:
www.searchpress com

For further inspiration:
– join the Half Yard Sewing Club:
www.halfyardsewingclub.com
– visit Debbie's YouTube channel:
www.youtube.com/user/thimblelane
– visit Debbie's website:
www.debbieshoresewing.com

Debbie Shore's
SEWING ROOM SECRETS
Machine Sewing

Top tips and techniques for
successful sewing

SEARCH PRESS

CONTENTS

ABOUT THIS BOOK

This book is for new sewers, or those coming back to sewing who are finding that things have changed somewhat over the years! It's for those of you who say, 'I've had a sewing machine for years and never taken it out of the box', or 'I'd love to be able to sew but I don't know where to start'.

I'll take you on a guided tour of my sewing room, stopping off to explore the tools and equipment I use, while sharing with you many hints and tips that I've picked up over the years I've been sewing.

Although I enjoy dressmaking and quilting, my passion is for craft items and home décor, which is why my books are filled with pillow covers, tea cosies, accessories for my sewing room and lots of handbags! These types of projects are perfect for a beginner: quick sews that are purposeful and can be gifted. So, to keep this book from becoming too heavy to lift off the shelf, I'm concentrating on these types of projects! However, I've included just a few dressmaking and quilting tips that may help if that's the journey you choose to take.

My aim is to give the nervous sewer the confidence to give it a go, to take away any fear of sewing machines and to give you a little inspiration to get started.

ABOUT ME

My mum was a seamstress, making clothes for me, my sister and other members of the family, particularly when a wedding was forthcoming! Our house was always busy with fittings, the drawers and cupboards were filled with fabrics and the sound of sewing machines revving and crisp scissors crunching through layers of fabric is still very nostalgic for me. Sewing was never my intended career, more of a hobby and necessity, particularly when I had kids of my own and alterations and repairs were the affordable way of keeping their wardrobes smart and up-to-date!

For over thirty years I have worked as a TV presenter, while still enjoying my sewing hobby in my spare time. A few years ago, several elements of my life started coming together… I was making up some cushion covers which I was so pleased with I asked my husband Garie, a fashion photographer, to take some pictures. I sent the projects off to Search Press, who produced my first book, *Making Cushion Covers*. This was the first of now seventeen sewing project books, and my own range of patterns and products, which I present on shopping TV.

So now my own cupboards are filled with fabrics and my home has the sound of revving sewing machines and crunching scissors. Who knows, in a few years' time my children may be saying the exact same thing!

MY QUICK TIPS

A few key sewing tips before you get started...

⊕ Invest in a lint roll, particularly if you're working with fabrics like corduroy and fleeces which tend to be magnets for dust, threads and cat hair!

⊕ Stick a tape measure along the front of your cutting table – it's a handy way to measure fabrics.

⊕ Steel wool stuffed inside a pincushion can help keep pins and needles sharp.

⊕ Occasionally cutting through aluminium foil will help to keep your scissors sharp.

⊕ Make the most of wall space: you'll be able to find items quickly, and it helps to keep your work space clear. Many quilters will have a sheet of natural wadding/batting on their wall. Patchwork pieces of fabric will stick to the fibres so that patterns can easily be arranged.

⊕ If you're having problems threading a hand-sewing needle, spray a little hairspray on your fingers and pass the thread through. When it dries, the end of the thread will be stiff enough to thread.

⊕ Use dental floss to hand sew buttons onto your projects: it's very strong, so you're less likely to lose a button!

⊕ Shorten your stitch length when sewing anything that will be stuffed, such as pincushions and soft toys, to help strengthen the stitch when under pressure.

⊕ Keep a magnet to hand for when you drop pins and needles on the floor!

⊕ When pinning fabric pieces, pin at a 90° angle to the raw edges with the pin heads sitting off the fabric. This way, it's easy to remove the pins as you sew, and if your machine needle accidentally hits a pin it's more likely to roll off it, instead of hitting the top of the pin which could break your needle.

⊕ Keep your sewing machine manual somewhere accessible. There are usually troubleshooting pages at the back which may come in handy!

⊕ Make sure there are no little 'nicks' on your thread spool. The thread could catch on these as you sew and may pull or even break your stitches.

Use a lint roll to clean up your fabric.

Insert pins at right angles to the fabric so they are easy to remove.

Cut through foil to keep your scissors sharp.

Use a magnet to pick up dropped needles and pins.

⊕ If you find your foot slips off your sewing machine pedal, wrap a couple of elastic bands around it to give it a bit of grip.

⊕ A straightforward way to gather fabric is to sew over a length of cord using a zigzag stitch, making sure you don't take the needle through the actual cord. Secure one end of the cord and pull the fabric back to gather!

⊕ Not sure which is the right side of plain fabric? Take a look at the selvedge. The hooks that stretch the fabric in the printing process go through the edges of the fabric from the back to front, so the front side will have little holes that appear rougher than the back.

⊕ When using adhesive sheets with intricate appliqué motifs, scratch the middle of the paper backing with a pin, and remove the backing from the centre. This will stop the paper tugging at the edge of the fabric which can cause it to fray.

⊕ Mark an accurate seam allowance by tying together two pencils. The distance between the two points will be 5mm (¼in). Pop another pencil in the middle and you'll have a 1.5cm (⅝in) seam allowance.

⊕ Toe separators are a perfect place for storing bobbins!

⊕ Sewing a straight line? Practice makes perfect. In the meantime, use the markings on the needle plate, or try putting masking tape or an elastic band over the bed of your machine and using this as a guide for the edge of your fabric.

⊕ To stop the ends of webbing bag straps from fraying, carefully and quickly singe the ends of the strap in a candle flame or lighter to melt the threads.

⊕ Avoid cutting wadding/batting with a rotary cutter and mat. The fibres of the fabric can be pushed into the cuts on the mat which can then be difficult to remove!

⊕ To prevent your thread from tangling, make sure you thread your needle (hand or machine) in the direction that the thread comes off the spool.

⊕ If you need to lift your sewing machine needle, always turn the hand wheel towards you to help protect the gears and mechanisms inside the machine.

⊕ When sewing seams such as the lining in a bag, I start at the cross section so that I can line the seams up precisely. Nobody notices a perfect seam, but they certainly notice a bad one!

See also the fabric terminology section, on pages 30–31.

Gathering with zigzag stitch over a length of cord.

Selvedges tell you which is the front of the fabric.

Toe separators are perfect for storing bobbins.

Singe webbing to stop it fraying.

Start seams at the cross section when sewing lining in a bag.

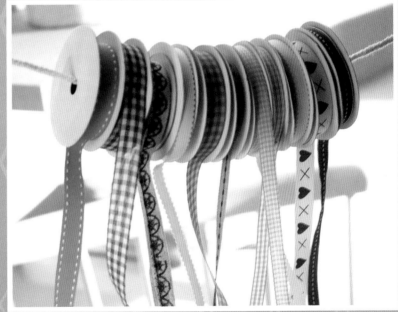

SEWING ROOM ESSENTIALS

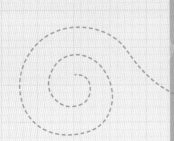

MY SEWING ROOM

I not only write books, but design patterns and projects, film video tutorials and supply photography, so although I work from home, I have four rooms dedicated to sewing. I don't have an enormous collection of sewing machines; the one I use every day is a professional, metal-cased machine that is very quick and will cope with everything I throw at it! Understandably, not everyone is in the market for such machines, so I also have a couple of regular domestic machines, electronic and computerized, as it's important that my projects can be sewn on any level of machine. I do, however, have quite a collection of vintage machines, purely because I love the nostalgic look of these beautiful works of engineering. I also have a four-thread overlocker/serger which I mainly use for dressmaking, and apart from my computer and printer, that's all the machinery I need.

Lighting is very important in my work area. As you can see below, my room is flooded with sunlight on a good day, but I also use daylight bulbs in several lamps around my room. Lamps on sewing machines are useful, but I find a bright light over my machine really helpful.

As I spend so much time at the machine, I use a chair with back support, at a height where my elbows are at right angles to the bed of my machine – the pillow gets me to the right height! Pets are a big part of my life so there's always a space for cats and dogs in my room.

I like to keep my room as tidy as I can; I work more efficiently when I'm organized. On the shelves are boxes of my most used folded fabric, sorted into colours.

My second room (see above) is used for filming, but when the cameras are off I use the space for cutting; the large table is perfect for keeping fabric flat and there is lots of shelved storage space.

Rooms three and four are for storage and photography; as you can imagine, I end up with many samples of my designs, all kept in boxes just in case I need them to dress the sets on TV or stands at shows.

Although I'd love to hoard fabric, I have to be quite ruthless in only keeping fabric I know will have a purpose, so any material that I've had for a few months will be bagged up and sent to schools and workshops, otherwise there would be no room left in the house for my family!

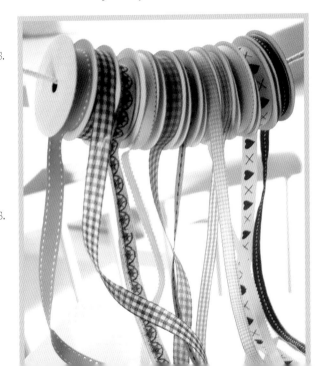

SEWING MACHINES

A sewing machine is probably the most expensive and most important sewing tool you'll buy, so take your time to choose the right model. It should last you for many years to come. There are two main types of machine: electronic and computerized. I would always recommend a computerized machine as they tend to have more features, more stitches and are generally easier to use. But let's get back to basics and talk about what sewing actually is and the role your machine will play.

Sewing is basically joining two or more pieces of fabric together with needle and thread. Using two threads, a motor and a series of gears and tensions, your machine will loop together the threads, one from the top of your machine and one from underneath, joining them in the middle of the layers of fabric. Most machines work in the same way, the big decision is which will best suit your needs. Here are a few pointers...

12

Looks are important, but check out all the features of that pretty machine before you buy! Some machines like this one will sew without a foot pedal – they use a stop/start button and speed control on the machine.

CHECKLIST FOR CHOOSING WHICH SEWING MACHINE TO BUY

⊕ Whatever machine you choose, go for a well-known brand which can offer a warranty and support. You're spending a considerable amount of money, so peace of mind is important.

⊕ What will you use your machine for? Dressmaking, patchwork, quilting, craft items, homewares, repairs – there are so many different sides to sewing. Maybe you have one use in mind, perhaps all of them. You may be surprised by the route your sewing journey takes you on, so try to future-proof yourself to a degree by buying a machine that you consider has a few too many features – you don't want to be upgrading your machine for a good while to come!

⊕ Budget obviously plays a large part – you normally get what you pay for with sewing machines, but don't overspend. Will you really use 300 stitches for example? As a beginner, you'll need a straight and zigzag stitch, and buttonholes are useful if you're a dressmaker. An automatic buttonhole function to fit the size of your buttons will give your projects the professional finish we're all aiming for. An over-edge stitch can help to stop your fabric from fraying and a few decorative stitches are fun. A budding dressmaker will use a blind hem stitch for hemming (you'll need a specific foot for this, see page 19). A patchworker may like more decorative stitches. Which leads onto my next point...

A needle up/down function is important for many sewers, enabling you to choose the needle position when you stop sewing. This makes pivoting simple, and is a must-have for patchworkers or those who enjoy appliqué.

I always look for a machine with a needle threader (a lever on the side of the machine that when pressed, takes a small hook through the eye of the needle, grabs the thread and pulls it through to form a loop). This is an invaluable feature for those who (like me) just can't see to thread a needle by hand!

If free-motion embroidery is on your to-do list, a drop feed dog facility is helpful, moving the grippers that feed the fabric under the machine out of the way so that you are able to move your work in any direction while sewing. Some machines come with a 'darning plate' which covers the feed dogs and disables them in the same way.

The more feet the better! Your machine will come with a standard/zigzag and a zipper foot, if it has buttonhole stitches there should be a buttonhole foot included. There are many extra feet available which all have specific jobs to do (see the section on feet on pages 17–19), but the more that are included with your machine, the fewer you have to buy!

If you'll be working with projects such as curtains or quilting, look for a machine with a large bed (see the diagram on page 14) that can take a greater bulk of fabric.

Some machines will have an extra high presser foot lever to lift the foot over thicker seams (such as those in jeans).

Where will you be storing your machine? Will you be taking it to workshops? If so, bear in mind the weight – there are some feature-packed compact machines on the market that will be easier to carry than a large, heavy machine.

When you've taken all things into consideration, it's worth a visit to your local dealer who should be able to advise you further and allow you to 'test drive' a few machines before making your decision. Alternatively, visit one of the many sewing exhibitions where you'll find a range of manufacturers displaying their machines. Again you'll be able to try them out and perhaps purchase at a favourable price!

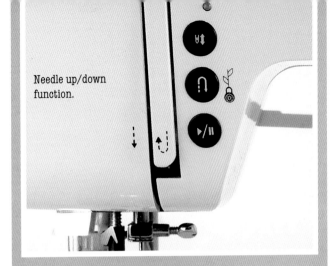
Needle up/down function.

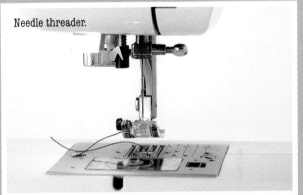
Needle threader.

Free-motion foot.

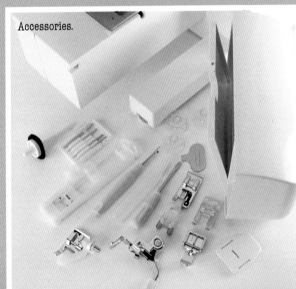
Accessories.

YOUR SEWING MACHINE

Once you've purchased your sewing machine, take the time to familiarize yourself with how it works. The picture below shows the main parts of a standard machine – all machines vary, but all will have these same basic functions.

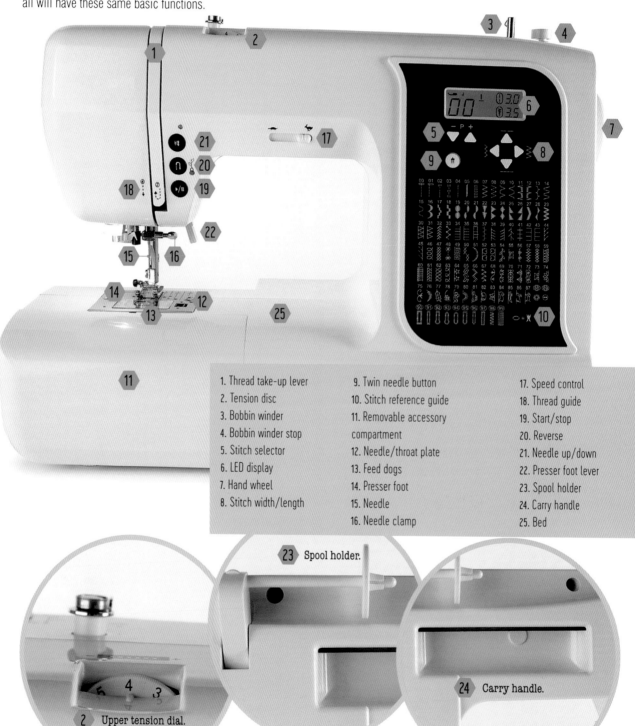

1. Thread take-up lever
2. Tension disc
3. Bobbin winder
4. Bobbin winder stop
5. Stitch selector
6. LED display
7. Hand wheel
8. Stitch width/length
9. Twin needle button
10. Stitch reference guide
11. Removable accessory compartment
12. Needle/throat plate
13. Feed dogs
14. Presser foot
15. Needle
16. Needle clamp
17. Speed control
18. Thread guide
19. Start/stop
20. Reverse
21. Needle up/down
22. Presser foot lever
23. Spool holder
24. Carry handle
25. Bed

23 Spool holder.

24 Carry handle.

2 Upper tension dial.

14

MAINTAINING YOUR MACHINE

To keep your sewing machine in good working order, I would suggest following these few simple guidelines. Just a little TLC now and then will ensure your machine will last a lifetime. It's also a good idea to read the manual before you start sewing, for guidance on how to thread your machine and what the different parts do.

⊕ Replace your needle after every large project or after about eight hours of sewing. You'll notice a difference with the quality of your stitches and the sound of your machine. Doing this at the same time you clean your machine is a good habit to get into.

⊕ Keep the dust cover on your machine when not in use. Wipe the outside of your machine clean with a barely damp cloth, then immediately afterwards with a dry cloth so there is no wetness on the machine.

⊕ Always refer to your sewing machine manual with regards to cleaning and oiling. On a regular basis, with your machine unplugged, unscrew the needle plate and remove the bobbin (1). Pick up any lint that has built up underneath with a small brush – most machines will come with a lint brush (2). Carefully remove the circular holder for the bobbin (the 'hook') and, again, pick up any build-up of lint (3). Don't be tempted to blow into your machine – moisture isn't welcome around metal parts!

⊕ If your machine comes with oil, check the manual – there may be a wick in the centre of the magnet that holds the hook in place. Pop a few drops of oil here (4).

Regularly unscrew the needle plate and remove the bobbin to check for lint that has collected underneath.

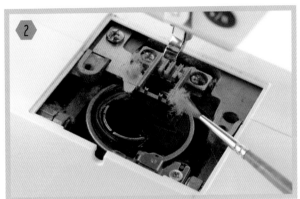

Use a small brush to collect any lint.

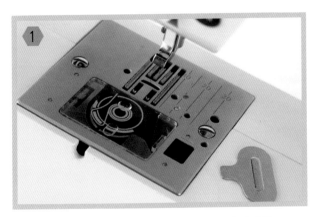

Remove the hook and pick up any lint that has collected.

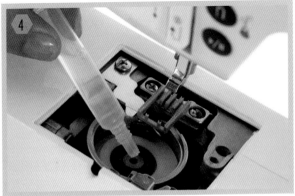

Add some oil to your machine as required.

WHEN THINGS GO WRONG

Two tips to start with: re-threading your machine will solve most of your stitching problems, and always make sure you have a clean, lint-free machine. But, if those don't work…

Thread breaking

⊕ Is your thread decent quality? Cheaper threads can be made from shorter fibres that can easily break.

⊕ Check the route of your thread. Occasionally it can become tangled in the threading system, particularly around the top of the take-up lever.

⊕ Check that the thread is coming off the spool smoothly. There are sometimes small nicks around the top of the spool that can catch the thread and eventually snap it.

⊕ If your thread is breaking at the needle, it may be too thick for the size of the needle, which will cause friction.

Stitches skipping

⊕ First, change the needle for a new one. There may be a slight bend in the needle, or it may be blunt.

⊕ Use the correct needle for the fabric you're working with (see page 20) and the same weight of thread on the top and bottom.

⊕ Re-thread the machine both top and bottom, just in case one of the threading stages has been missed.

⊕ Don't pull or push your fabric through the machine, that's the job of the feed dogs!

Thread knotting at the start of your sewing

⊕ If your thread knots as you start to sew from the edge of the fabric, or even jams the edge of the fabric into the feed dogs, carefully snip away the knotted thread. In some cases you may need to unscrew the throat plate to clear the jam (always switch off the machine first).

When you're ready to sew again, start the stitch line a little way from the edge, making sure both threads are to the back. Reverse back to the edge (it may help to hold the threads with your left hand), then sew forwards again. The same applies when you come to the end of your stitching – stop shortly before the edge of your fabric, reverse a couple of stitches then sew off the fabric.

Thread bunching under your fabric

⊕ If it looks like a bird's nest under your work, there's a problem with the top thread. Make sure the tension is engaged by taking the thread as far as the needle, then putting the presser foot down. It should be quite difficult to pull the thread through if it is passing through the tension discs correctly.

Thread bunching on top of your fabric

⊕ This is a bobbin tension problem. Take out the bobbin and re-thread, making sure the thread passes through the grooves in the side of the bobbin holder. Check that the bobbin is sitting in the holder the right way round, usually with the thread coming off the bottom of the bobbin. Check your user manual if you're not sure.

Needle not picking up the bobbin thread

⊕ Check that your needle is pushed into the needle holder as far as it will go. After a few hours of sewing it may have worked loose and dropped down a little.

⊕ Is your needle fitted the right way round? Most domestic machines will take the flat part of the needle to the back of the holder.

Fabric slipping

⊕ If your machine has a presser foot pressure dial, try increasing the pressure slightly. Alternatively, invest in a walking foot to help feed the fabric through the machine from the top as well as the bottom.

SEWING MACHINE FEET

A presser foot is an attachment that keeps your fabric flat as the sewing machine feeds the fabric under the needle. There are many presser feet available for your sewing machine, each with a unique job to do, making sewing techniques easier and your finished work look professional. Most domestic sewing machine feet will clip onto an adaptor (sometimes called an 'ankle') on the end of the take-up lever (see the diagram on page 14); some you will need to screw on.

Your sewing machine will come with a few feet included. Below are listed some of the most used feet and extra feet you may wish to invest in. There are many other types of feet available for gathering, adding bias binding, ruffling, applying cord, elastic and beads but I think the ones below are the feet you'll use the most. Presser feet may vary in appearance from one manufacturer to another – always buy the recommended feet for your machine.

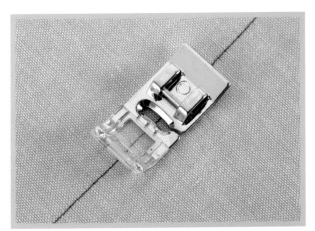

Standard/zigzag foot

This foot will be fitted to your machine when you first take it out of the box. It will have a wide hole for the needle to pass through and enable it to 'swing' from side to side when using zigzag or decorative stitches without the needle hitting the foot. This is the foot you'll use for most of your projects.

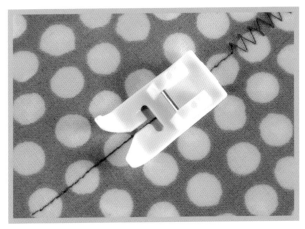

Zipper foot

The open sides of this foot allow the needle to sew close to the edge of the foot and therefore close to the teeth of a zip. This is also useful for making piping (see page 59) or top-stitching close to interruptions such as fastenings.

Non-stick foot

If you're sewing laminated fabric or leather, you'll need a non-stick foot to help reduce friction, allowing the fabric to pass under the presser foot smoothly.

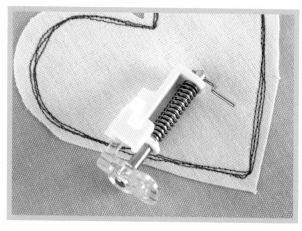

Free-motion/darning foot

This is another foot that is usually screwed onto the take-up lever. As with the walking foot, there is a bar that sits over the needle clamp. This makes the foot 'hop' across your fabric as you sew. Most darning feet have an open section and some will be clear plastic.

Button placement foot

The blue/green rubbery end of this foot grips onto the button to stop it slipping as you sew. Many machines have a specific stitch for sewing on buttons, stopping the feed dogs from doing their job of moving the fabric. After all, you don't want the button to move as you sew or you could break a needle.

If you don't have a button placement stitch, drop your feed dogs (or cover them with a darning plate) and use a zigzag stitch.

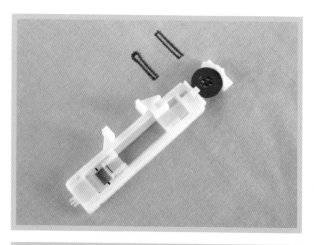

Buttonhole foot

Some buttonhole feet have a chamber at the back of the foot in which you fit the button you're using, enabling the machine to measure the size of buttonhole required, for a perfect fit every time. These usually feature on computerized machines with a one-step buttonhole stitch. Look out for a lever at the side of the machine that you need to pull down before starting to sew. This bar sits in between two posts on the foot, and instructs the machine when the buttonhole is stitched to the correct size. All you need to do now is to choose the style of buttonhole, press 'start' and the machine will complete the sewing in one step. Some machines have a four-step buttonhole, so you'll need to gauge the size of hole needed then stitch the four sides of the buttonhole separately. The little spike on the ends of the feet is designed to wrap cord around to create stronger buttonholes.

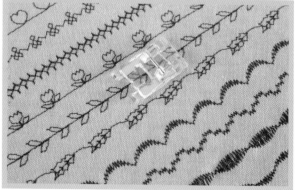

Satin stitch foot

This foot has two ski-like panels on the bottom, to raise the foot over satin stitches which are usually quite three-dimensional as the needle takes the thread over the same spot a few times. These feet are usually transparent so you can see the exact position of the stitch.

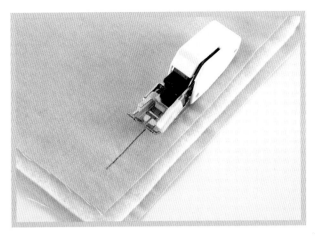

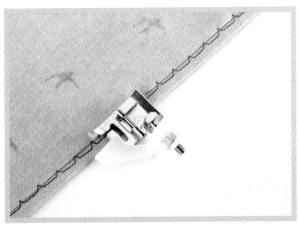

Walking foot

This is one of the feet you'll need to screw on. Take off the 'ankle' by unscrewing it (make sure you put it somewhere safe!) then attach the walking foot to the side of the take-up lever, making sure the bar at the side sits on top of the needle clamp. The motion of the needle going up and down activates the grippers on the bottom of the foot, feeding the fabric through evenly from both the top and bottom. A must-have for quilters who will be working with layers of fabric and wadding/batting, and for those of us sewing together different weights of fabric such as curtains with lining, or slippery fabrics like velvet and satin. Don't be concerned about the noise: the mechanism inside the foot can make your machine sound a little louder than usual!

Blind hem/invisible hem foot

Although you can sew a blind hem without the foot, an adjustable blind hem foot makes sewing so much easier as there is a guide for the fold in your fabric to run against to help form a perfect hem. You'll also find this foot useful when sewing on appliqué – keep the edge of the appliqué shape butted up against the guide to keep an even seam allowance.

Over-edge foot

Use this foot with an over-edge stitch to take the thread around the raw edge of your fabric. The foot has a blade-like prong that helps to tuck in stray threads.

Rolled hem foot

Feed the edge of your fabric through the coil on this foot and as you sew, you'll create a fine hem of about 4.5cm (1¾in). Perfect for very fine fabrics for items such as wedding veils.

SEWING MACHINE NEEDLES

Needles are sized in metric and imperial. The smaller the number the finer the needle, and the size of a needle is calculated by its diameter; for example an 80 needle is 0.8mm in diameter. Understanding needles and their associated numbers will help you to make the correct choice for your fabric and thread, resulting in perfect seams.

These are my most-used needles:

Size 10 /70 organza, silk
Size 11 /75 lingerie, satin
Size 12 /80 taffeta, quilt cotton, lining fabric, voile, jersey
Size 14 /90 jeans and heavy cotton, linen
Size 16 /100 velvet, lace
Size 18 /110 wool, upholstery fabric, faux leather, laminates, twill
Size 20 /120 thick denim, canvas, heavy faux leather

Needles for specific fabrics and threads

A denim needle isn't just for denim; it's a strong needle with a very sharp point, making it suitable for thick fabrics.

A stretch or ball-point needle has a slightly rounded tip, allowing it to part the threads of knitted fabric such as jersey, instead of tearing through it. Sewing stretch fabric with a regular needle can result in skipped stitches.

A metallic needle has an elongated eye that allows metallic threads to pass through with minimal friction.

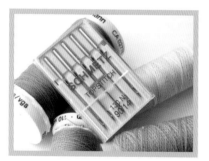

A top-stitch needle has an extra large eye to accommodate thick threads.

An embroidery needle has a long groove and large eye which allows delicate embroidery threads to pass through easily and reduce friction.

A universal needle can be used on knit or woven fabrics, so these will be your go-to needles if you're not sure of the fibre content of your fabric. It's so frustrating if you need a new needle halfway through a project and you don't have any in your sewing kit, so invest in a few packets!

A leather needle has an angled point that makes a tiny slit instead of a round hole, to help the thread pass smoothly through leather, suede and imitations.

SEWING WITH A TWIN NEEDLE

A twin needle is constructed of two needles that are joined with one shank, which fits into the needle holder on your sewing machine in the same way as your standard needle. When using a straight stitch, you'll see two rows of stitches on the top, while underneath the single thread from the bobbin zigzags from one row of stitches to the other, making this a perfect way to hem stretch fabrics.

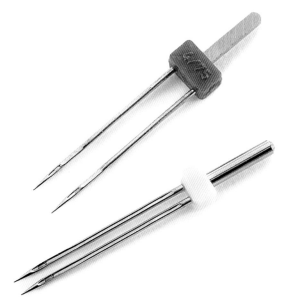

The needles come in sizes from 1.6mm to 6mm, which is the distance between the two needles. The wider needles are more suited to hemming. If you're using stretch fabric then make sure you use a twin stretch needle, as these have slightly rounded points to help prevent tearing the threads in the fabric.

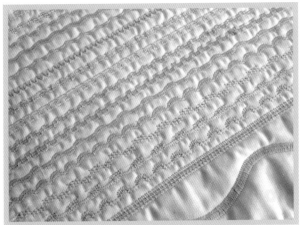

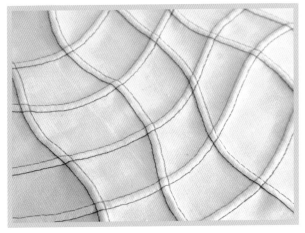

Pass the thread through the normal channels until you reach the needles, then thread each individually by hand (your needle threader won't work with a twin needle). Many sewing machines will have a selection button for twin needle sewing, preventing you from using unsuitable stitches such as buttonholes. If you're using a decorative stitch and you don't have this function, test the stitch first by turning the hand wheel slowly, to make sure that the needles don't hit the sides of the foot as they swing from side to side. If the stitch is too wide this could result in broken needles!

Always practise on a scrap piece of fabric first, as some decorative stitches work better than others.

Use a grooved pin tucking foot in combination with your twin needle to create pin tucks to decorate blouses, dresses or pillow covers. The grooves in the presser foot act as guides for parallel sewing. You may need to increase the tension on your sewing machine to create a raised line of fabric between the lines. Cord can be used under the rows of stitches to raise them even more.

There's nothing to say that pin tucks must be sewn in straight lines!

TOOLS

SCISSORS

Second in importance after your sewing machine are your scissors. I'd recommend four pairs to start with: fabric shears, embroidery scissors, pinking shears and paper scissors. Many are available for both left- and right-handed use, some with soft grip handles, some with a spring-action that help to open the blades after each cut to help reduce hand strain. A good pair of scissors can last you a lifetime so don't scrimp on price, and make sure you take care of them.

⊕ **Fabric shears** have a small handle for the thumb and a larger handle for the fingers, giving you the best possible grip for efficient cutting. The handles will be slightly bent, allowing the entire length of the blades to sit flat on the fabric as you cut. The blades will be 18cm (7in) or longer, and this is a good length for craft projects. If you're making curtains or larger items, choose larger blades such as 23 or 25cm (9 or 10in).

⊕ A pair of small, sharp **embroidery scissors** is essential for snipping into curves and corners and trimming threads. Thread snips are available that have sprung blades and very sharp points to allow you to trim the thread close to your fabric.

⊕ The blades on **pinking shears** make small zigzag cuts; the 45° angle of the cut helps to prevent woven fabrics from fraying, making it a quick way to finish seams. They are also useful for trimming seams around curves, an alternative way of 'snipping into curves'. Used on non-woven fabric such as felt, a decorative effect is created.

⊕ Unlike shears, the handles on **paper scissors** tend to be the same size, making them suitable for both left- and right-handed use. Keep these scissors for pattern cutting, and if a member of your family needs to borrow some, hand them these, not your shears!

Paper scissors.

22

Fabric shears.

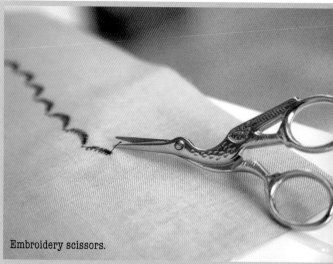

Embroidery scissors.

Pinking shears.

CARING FOR YOUR SCISSORS

⊕ Try not to use your fabric scissors for cutting paper. Cutting through tissue pattern paper won't damage your shears, but continuously cutting through paper and card can eventually blunt them.

⊕ If your scissors need sharpening I'd recommend taking them to a professional to avoid damaging the blades – an unskilled sharpener can do more harm than good!

⊕ If they came with a sheath, get into the habit of covering the blades when you've finished with them. This can not only help to protect the blades from damage, but help to protect you from damage if the scissors are accidentally knocked off the table! If you don't have a sheath, make one yourself (see page 50).

⊕ Don't store your scissors in a drawer, as rummaging round a crowded drawer can scratch and nick the blades. If they need to be out of the way try hanging them on hooks or even a mug tree!

⊕ Avoid moisture! Never cut through wet fabric, and if you wipe your scissors clean make sure you wipe them dry afterwards.

⊕ Hairdressing suppliers can provide scissor oil. Rub a little into the screw area to lubricate, wiping it all away before using again. Make a few cuts on scrap fabric before using your scissors after oiling to make sure.

⊕ Don't drop your scissors – even the toughest blades can be knocked out of alignment. I found this out by accidentally dropping an expensive pair of fabric shears on a carpeted floor: they landed on their point which made only a slight buckle in the blades but rendered them useless. (At least they missed my feet as they fell!)

⊕ Be aware that some ribbons are wired; don't try to cut across the teeth of metal zips; remove any pins from your cutting line – and if you're re-purposing garments such as jeans, avoid metal rivets!

23

PINS

⊕ I use glass-head pins for most of my projects for two reasons: first, they can be seen if I drop them, and second, the glass ball on the end of the pin won't melt if touched by a hot iron. They are 3.5cm (1⅜in) long and the shaft is made from strong nickel-plated steel so they don't easily bend.

⊕ Flower-head pins are long and fine, useful for multiple layers of fabric when quilting, with brightly coloured flat heads that again can easily be seen!

⊕ As a basic rule of thumb, use a fine pin for delicate fabrics and long pins for heavy fabric and layers. If in doubt, check the packaging; the label should describe what materials the pins have been designed for.

FABRIC CLIPS

⊕ These are a suitable alternative to pins, especially when working with heavy fabrics, thick layers of fabric or piping that can be difficult to pin, or laminates where pins may leave holes. They come in numerous colours and sizes and some manufacturers will add seam allowance markings on the flat side. Remove the clips as you sew.

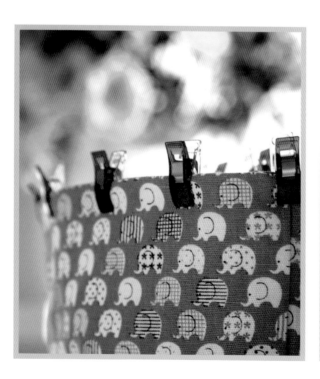

PINCUSHIONS

⊕ There are pincushions for the wrist, for your sewing machine, on the lids of jam jars and sewing boxes, patchworked, vintage, large, small and even novelty pincushions in the form of anything from hedgehogs to fruit. It's your choice! I like a pincushion that can accommodate my glass- and flower-head pins, machine- and hand-sewing needles and a few safety pins too. A sturdy base prevents it from rolling across my table, and I push my doll needles straight through the centre of the long body of the pincushion to protect them from breakage. Here's something you may not know: the little strawberry that is attached to many tomato-shaped pincushions is filled with sand to help keep your pins sharp! (See the pincushion project on page 50.)

24

HAND-SEWING NEEDLES

⊕ Needles vary in length, point shape and thickness depending on their purpose. I'd suggest keeping a pack of sharps in various sizes in your sewing kit for general use. The smaller the size of the needle the thicker it will be, so a size 1 needle will be quite thick compared to a size 12 which will be finer. The eye of the needle should be large enough to accommodate your thread, but don't be tempted to use a large-eyed needle with fine thread, or the needle will leave holes in your work.

If you're working with stretch fabric, choose a ball-point needle. These have a slightly rounded tip that separates the yarns of the fabric instead of cutting through them, helping to prevent laddering.

I have a few doll needles, which are very long needles that I use not just for doll making, but for pushing through the centre of pillows when adding buttons.

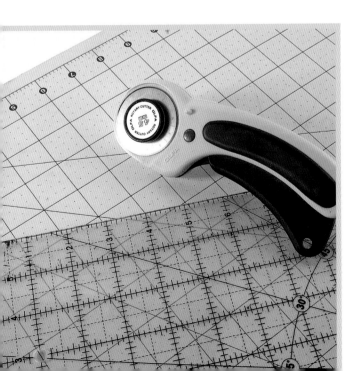

ROTARY CUTTER, RULER AND MAT

I've grouped these three items as they go hand in hand. I use this method of cutting probably more than I use scissors, certainly for cutting quick, accurate straight lines.

⊕ A 45mm-blade rotary cutter is the most useful size and many rotary cutters can be adjusted for left- or right-handed cutting. Always cover the blade with a safety guard after every cut (this will soon become a habit), as these blades are incredibly sharp. It is easy to ruin a blade by accidentally cutting over a stray pin, so make sure your cutting mat is clear of anything metal.

28mm cutters are useful for cutting around curves or following templates and 60mm blades will make light work of multiple layers of fabric or larger projects such as curtains. Always dispose of the blades safely – even a blade that you'd consider to be blunt can still be dangerous.

⊕ Choose a 61 × 15cm (24 × 6in) ruler with 3mm (1/8in) increments. You'll find 30°, 45° and 60° markings useful for measuring on the bias or marking grids on your fabric for quilting. Some rulers are frosted so that the grid lines stand out against your fabric; some have markings in black and white for the same reason. The ruler you use with a rotary cutter should be at least 3mm (1/8in) thick to help stop the blade from slipping over the ruler when cutting.

There are many shapes and sizes of rulers and quilting templates available to buy, but for the beginner sewer this one ruler should suit most projects.

⊕ You'll need a mat to protect both your table and the blade of your rotary cutter, the larger the better! If you're taking a mat to a workshop you may wish to invest in two: a large one for your sewing room and a smaller, more portable size for classes. Some mats will be in inches on one side and centimetres on the other, with many diagonal markings for bias cutting and measuring angles. Try to store your mat flat when not in use to prevent it buckling, and keep it clean – I've spoiled a straight cut in the past by not removing a blob of glue which dried hard!

A self-healing cutting mat is a worthwhile investment – the cuts you make simply close over, prolonging the life of your mat. These mats tend to grip your fabric slightly, unlike hard plastic mats, and there's less chance of your blade slipping. These mats benefit from moisture so cleaning with warm water occasionally is a good idea, and rotate the mat every now and again to avoid cutting on the same spot over and over again.

IRON

An iron is an essential tool for a successful sewer. I iron the creases out of tissue paper patterns, iron my fabric flat before cutting, and press my seams, pleats and darts. Give a blast of steam from your iron to pre-shrink fabric instead of washing, and always iron a patch test on scrap fabric first to make sure you have the correct heat setting.

You'll notice I mentioned 'pressing' and 'ironing' – they are two very different things. Pressing is the motion of putting the iron over the fabric then lifting it, preventing the seam distorting, whereas ironing is a sweeping motion. To keep it simple, seams are set by pressing, creases removed by ironing. Personally, I prefer a steam-generator iron that has been designed to be left on for extended periods of time; an automatic shut off is a bonus! A choice of steam or no steam is important, and make sure you can regulate the temperature according to the fibre content of your fabric.

For small projects, I keep a travel iron next to my sewing table, with a small ironing pad that can be folded away after use.

BAMBOO POINTER AND CREASER

A perfect little tool for pushing out points and corners without making holes in your fabric (ever tried using the points of scissors? Enough said…) and pressing the occasional seam open on small projects.

SEAM RIPPER

Your sewing machine may come with a seam ripper but these little tools will blunt over time, so keep a few in stock as you don't want to be without them. Wonky stitching can happen to the best of us, so a seam ripper/quick unpick/stitch picker can make light work of undoing our small mistakes. They are also useful for cutting buttonholes and fitting bag closures. Did you know that the red plastic ball on some seam rippers is there to protect your fabric as you tear through the stitches? Place the tool ball side down and the small blade will glide through seams.

THIMBLE

Protect your finger as you hand sew with a thimble. I prefer leather thimbles as they are comfortable and don't allow the needle to slip.

BODKIN

This is a thick needle with a large eye and a ball on the pointed end, used to thread ribbon or elastic into projects and garments.

TWEEZERS

I use tweezers to pick up small embellishments such as sequins and beads, and to hold anything I'm fixing with my hot glue gun to keep my fingers away from the glue! You can also use them to pick up tiny threads, and grab the end of a tube of fabric that needs turning. If you don't have a needle threader on your sewing machine they are useful to hold your thread as you push it through the eye of the needle.

26

Different styles of bodkin.

ADHESIVES

I keep a good selection of adhesives in my store cupboard: temporary and permanent, fabric and paper, they're all useful. If you're using any kind of adhesive with machine-sewn projects, make sure they are suitable for use with machines. You don't want to cause any damage to your sewing machine by getting glue inside it.

⊕ **Temporary or repositionable adhesive** comes in wet, spray or stick form. I use spray to hold appliqué shapes in place while sewing, and it keeps layers of fabric and wadding/batting from puckering under the machine, making it a quick and easy option for assembling your 'quilt sandwich'. Wet tacking/basting glues are a good alternative to pins for appliqué and zip insertion. My glue sticks are used mostly when I'm English paper piecing.

⊕ There are various types of **permanent adhesives**. Spray adhesive is applied to the wrong side of your fabric, and is adhered to your project when ironed, enabling you to fuse wadding/batting and add patches for repairs. Use a strong, wet fabric glue to hold purses in frames, and add embellishments and bows to projects such as bags that don't need to be laundered. I like to add a dot of glue behind buttons on items like soft toys, as an extra assurance that little hands won't be able to pull them off!

⊕ **Fusible adhesive** comes as sheets of glue that are ironed to the wrong side of your fabric. The paper backing is then removed and the fabric re-ironed into position. Used for appliqué, it's a great way to prevent fraying and puckering and in some cases you may not even need to sew! You can draw onto the paper backing before cutting out your shapes, using patterns, templates or drawing free hand. Bear in mind that, as you're drawing on the back of the fabric, letters and numbers will need to be reversed.

⊕ I use my **hot glue gun** for crafty projects such as adding flowers and bows to a wreath, or adding trim to a lampshade or sewing box. Sticks of glue are pushed into the back of the gun, which heats them up and melts them so that when the trigger is pulled, hot glue comes out of the nozzle. The glue dries very quickly, and be careful as it is also incredibly hot! It sometimes leaves very fine strands of glue over your work which can easily be removed with a heat gun. If you don't have a heat gun simply peel them away using your tweezers.

Temporary adhesives.

Permanent adhesives.

Hot glue gun.

FABRICS

Without filling too many pages of this book with the technicalities of fabric construction, I thought I'd keep it simple and just give you an overview of the fabrics I use most.

COTTON

Breathable, natural, and available in almost every colour and print you'll ever need, cotton is certainly the fabric of choice for most of my projects, whether that's bags, dresses, curtains or soft furnishings. Cotton is the quilter's choice of fabric and is perfect for both hand sewing and machine sewing. It's available in many different weights and weaves that create texture and thickness, making it suitable for drapery, attire and bed linen. It's always best to pre-wash cotton to allow for shrinkage, but if you're impatient, give the fabric a blast of steam from your iron and that should do the trick!

DENIM

A sturdy cotton that creates a diagonal weave, making it a perfect casual fabric for bags and jeans. Denim tends to fade and soften after washing; look for worn jeans in charity shops to cut up for your projects.

CORDUROY/NEEDLECORD

Another cotton fabric, this time with velvety rows that create a ribbed effect. A lovely soft fabric for craft items or dressmaking.

POLY-COTTON

The best of both worlds for dressmakers, a combination of natural and artificial fibres makes for a strong, colour-fast, easy to launder material that won't need to be pre-washed.

WOOL

Another natural fabric that can be woven or knitted, and used for anything from coats to pillows to bags. Although some wools can be washed, it's best to spot clean them or have them professionally dry cleaned. Remove wrinkles with steam rather than ironing.

29

LAMINATE

Laminated fabric is usually cotton coated with a wipe-clean layer on one side, making it a good choice for bags, raincoats, baby changing mats and tablecloths. It is available in many fun prints and colours and the coating prevents it from fraying. To sew you'll need a non-stick foot on your sewing machine, and pins will leave holes so piece together with fabric clips (see page 24). Don't put it in the washing machine or tumble dryer and use a warm iron only on the uncoated back of the fabric.

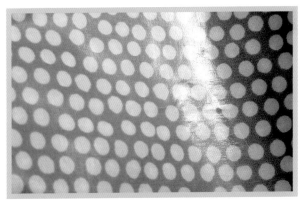

FLEECE

A knitted polyester fabric which has a 'pile' or 'nap' on one side, this doesn't fray but may shed slightly as you cut it. It is a soft fabric that children will love to cuddle, either in the form of soft toys or blankets.

FABRIC TERMINOLOGY

BOLT

A bolt is simply the cardboard block that fabric is wound around. Most commonly this will be quilting or craft cotton, folded in half (wrong sides together). Take a look at the end of the bolt before you buy – there is important information there regarding the fabric content, manufacturer, width of fabric and price.

GRAIN

This describes the direction of woven threads. The lengthways grain is parallel to the selvedge (see page 31), running the length of the fabric. The crosswise grain runs from side to side (selvedge to selvedge). The bias grain is at a 45° angle diagonally across the fabric. Cutting your fabric on the grain ensures you achieve the best drape for dressmaking and curtains, but for smaller crafty projects this isn't so important. Curtains not cut on the grain tend to twist. I found this with some shop-bought curtains, and no amount of pressing would make them hang straight.

The bias grain has the most stretch, making it perfect for binding and piping. Skirt and dress patterns sometimes require the fabric to be cut on the bias to add a little 'give' to the garment.

PRE-CUTS

If you add up the yardage, packs of pre-cut fabrics can work out to be more expensive than buying by the yard, but the benefit of buying these packs is that you have samples of a wide range of colours and prints of fabric that you know will match.

FAT QUARTERS AND EIGHTHS

A yard of fabric from the roll will most commonly measure 112 × 92cm (44 × 36in). Cut in half widthways and lengthways and you'll have four equal pieces measuring 56 × 46cm (22 × 18in). These are fat quarters.

Cut in half again and, depending on which way you cut, these pieces will measure either 28 × 46cm (11 × 18in) or 56 × 23cm (22 × 9in). These are fat eighths.

Fat sixteenths aren't so common, but are half the fat eighth, measuring 28 × 23cm (11 × 9in).

As your fabric comes off the roll, cut a strip measuring 112 × 23cm (44 × 9in). This is a long quarter.

112cm (44in)

92cm (36in)

Fat quarter
56x46cm
(22x18in)

Fat quarter
56x46cm
(22x18in)

Fat eighth
28x46cm
(11x18in)

Fat eighth
28x46cm
(11x18in)

Fat eighth
56x23cm
(22x9in)

Fat eighth
56x23cm
(22x9in)

A yard of fabric

RIGHT/WRONG SIDES

The right side of your fabric is the side you want to see. This is quite clear on a printed fabric as the right side will be brighter than the wrong side. With some fabrics, it can be difficult to determine which is right and wrong as the two look very similar. A rule of thumb is to look at the little holes in the selvedge. These holes are made by small hooks that hold the fabric on rollers as it goes through various processes; they push through the fabric from the back to the front, making the holes on the right side slightly raised. Run your finger over them: the rougher side will be the right side. If this doesn't work and you really can't tell the difference, then the chances are that nobody else will. Just make sure you use the same side for each part of your project, so mark one side with either safety pins or chalk.

ROLL

Furnishing and dressmaking fabric usually comes on a roll, with the fabric information on a swing tag. The width of the fabric varies; some may be folded in half. You may find it useful to take a picture of the tag, particularly if it has washing instructions or in case you need to buy more of the same fabric.

SELVEDGE

The selvedges are the edges either side of the fabric as it comes off the roll – tightly woven strips that prevent the fabric from unravelling or fraying. Sometimes they are printed with the name of the manufacturer, sometimes there will be coloured dots that refer to the colours of the print. Although you don't use the selvedges as they are usually a tighter weave than the fabric and may have small holes in them, it's a good idea to save a small piece in case you need to colour match your fabrics. Cut off the selvedges before you start your sewing projects but don't throw them away. Some selvedges are quite pretty and can be used as trimmings.

SQUARES

Packs of square pieces of fabric come in sizes from 2.5cm (1in) to 25cm (10in) and everything in between! These pre-cut squares of perfectly blended colours save you the job of cutting, so you can get on with the enjoyable bit, the sewing! You will typically find forty-two squares in a pack.

STRIPS

Sometimes rolled up together (see below), strips of coordinating fabrics usually measure 112 × 6.5cm (44 × 2½in). They are useful for patchworkers who will either sew together the strips or cut them into shapes to be joined back together again to create patterns. The number of strips in each pack varies from around twenty to forty.

WARP AND WEFT

This is the same as the grain; the warp is lengthways and the weft is widthways (think 'weft to right'…).

WADDING

Choosing wadding/batting can be a bit of a minefield, so let's keep it simple. Traditionally, wadding is the padded layer that goes between the outer and lining fabrics of quilts, but I use it in bag making, table runners, tea cosies and any project that needs a touch of luxury or added drape.

Read the manufacturer's instructions regarding pre-washing, shrinkage and quilting distance. Terms you may see are 'loft', which is the thickness of the wadding, and 'scrim', which is the polyester layer that holds some natural waddings together.

For my projects I tend to just use fusible fleece and cotton wadding/batting for bags and quilts, but I thought you may find it useful to know the variations between the different types.

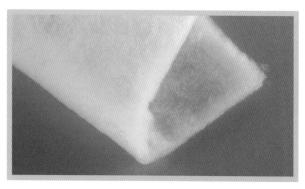

⊕ Synthetic **polyester** wadding/batting tends to have a high loft so is thicker than the natural alternative. Nowadays you can even find synthetic wadding/batting made from recycled plastic bottles!

⊕ **Natural** wadding/batting is made from cotton, wool, silk bamboo or soya, all usually softer and more breathable than synthetic. Cotton is ideal for quilts because of its high thermal value.

⊕ **Polyester-cotton** wadding/batting is usually eighty per cent cotton and twenty per cent polyester, forming a high-loft layer with the benefits of both materials, making it stable, warm but not weighty, and usually washable.

⊕ **Wool** wadding/batting is breathable, thermal and easily retains its loft, but may not be suitable for projects intended for regular use as it usually needs to be hand washed and dried flat.

⊕ **Bamboo, silk and cotton** can be blended together to form a warm, luxurious wadding which is particularly strong.

⊕ Choose a **fusible fleece** that is ironed onto the back of your fabric to give it form and stability. If you can't find fusible, use a sew-in wadding and try a spray of repositionable adhesive to hold it in place while sewing.

⊕ Also available on the market is an insulated, **thermal** wadding/batting which I use for oven gloves, tea cosies and mug hugs, to help keep my cuppa warm.

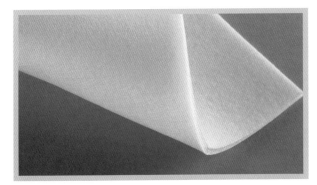

⊕ The new kid on the block is **foam stabilizer**, available to either fuse or sew in, which adds a real firmness to your project while remaining easy to sew through. Perfect if you want the item to stand up alone and keep its shape, you may need to trim it back to the seams to reduce bulk.

⊕ The term **'needle-punched'** simply means that the wadding/batting has been felted, by punching barbed needles through the material to help keep it stable.

INTERFACING

Interfacing is used to add firmness to fabric and is available to iron on or sew in. The iron-on interfacing has glue dots on one side and is fused to the wrong side of your fabric when ironed. It's not suitable for very fine fabrics as the glue could show through or the fabric may not tolerate heat, in which case use the sew-in version.

The weight of interfacing should be no heavier than the fabric. You can choose from woven, which should be cut on the grain as you would your fabric, non-woven which is suitable for most projects, or knitted for stretch fabrics. You could use a woven or non-woven interfacing on stretch fabric to stop it stretching.

Top: Interfacing is available in black or white for use on dark or light fabrics.

Above: If I'm making a bag that I need to feel firm I'll use a thick fusible interfacing that has a leather-like feel. Only use this for large bags as it can be quite difficult to work with.

INTERLINING

This is a layer of material that sits in between outer fabric and lining to add warmth, body and drape – think luxurious curtains and winter jackets. Interlining is sewn into the seams. Some curtain lining comes with interlining already bonded to one side.

STABILIZER

Designed to support fabric under the stresses of stitching, stabilizers are predominantly used in embroidery as temporary sheets either on top or underneath the fabric. Tear-away stabilizer is kept in place by the embroidery hoop and is ripped away when the project is finished; soluble stabilizer melts away in warm water; cut-away stabilizer is trimmed with scissors so a certain amount will remain in the stitches. Unlike interfacing, lightweight fabrics normally require heavy stabilizers, and heavy fabrics need lightweight support.

THREADS

There are so many threads on the market in such a range of materials, it can be hard to know where to start. So here's a little information that may make your choice of thread easier. I always recommend a decent-quality thread, but what makes thread good quality? It's mainly the strength, called 'tensile' strength, which helps to lengthen the life of your seams.

Look for a smooth thread. Your thread will be travelling through the eye of your needle at high speed and uneven thread can affect its strength and may even twist. In extreme cases, it could even wear your tension discs. Inexpensive thread could also have rough filaments that build up inside your sewing machine.

It is recommended that you try to use the same fibre content as your fabric – cotton with cotton, polyester with synthetic, etc. – although I don't always follow the rules. There are also different weights of threads to consider. Here are the basics:

⊕ Cotton thread is the most used natural fibre, favoured by quilters. However, synthetic thread tends to be stronger and more resistant to colour fading. The best of both worlds comes in corespun thread, with a polyester core and cotton fibres wrapped around it.

⊕ Silk thread is very thin so won't make holes in fine fabrics, making it also useful for tacking/basting tailored items.

⊕ Top-stitching thread is a thick, strong polyester thread used for stitching that can be seen on top of your work (e.g. on jeans) and is perfect for sewing buttonholes.

⊕ Metallic thread is a decorative rayon fibre that can be used with both your sewing machines and embroidery machines. You will benefit from investing in a metallic needle, which has a smooth coating around the eye to help stop friction from the metallic threads and therefore prevent breakage.

⊕ Embroidery thread is usually made from rayon as it's reflective and fine, designed to really show off your decorative stitches.

⊕ Thread weights can be confusing but, put simply, a smaller weight number (wt) depicts a heavier thread. As a rough guide, choose a 40wt for quilting, 50wt or 60wt for appliqué and filling your bobbin. 20–30wt is a thick thread for top-stitching and decorative work. If your thread weight looks like a fraction, i.e. 60/2, the first number is the weight and the second is how many strands in the thread. If you're still confused then choose an all-purpose 50wt which should work with most of your projects.

⊕ My main advice when buying thread would be to avoid threads that look 'fluffy' as this can be a sign of poor quality, and invest in as many colours as you can so that you never have to compromise!

TOY FILLER FOR SOFTIES

By 'softies' I mean toys, doorstops, draught excluders, pincushions, decorative items and anything that involves stuffing.

⊕ There are many different types of stuffing on the market – **polyester** is the most affordable and is available in different weights. The denser the stuffing the heavier it will be, so take into consideration what your project requires. You may want a doorstop to be firm and have extra weight, whereas a soft toy may require lighter stuffing.

⊕ **Organic stuffing** may be more suited to baby toys. Check if it's pre-shrunk, is washable and suitable for children.

⊕ You could also try **pellets**, particularly to add weight, but not for toys just in case the seams split…

⊕ Scraps of **fabric** can be torn into strips and used as stuffing, but may not feel very soft, so avoid using them for toys.

⊕ Below is my old teddy bear, stuffed with **wood wool**, which is still available and is used as a traditional stuffing for modern-day bears too. Also useful for stuffing tailor's hams as it absorbs moisture from the iron.

A FEW SOFTIE-MAKING TIPS

⊕ It helps to use tweezers to push toy filler into tube shapes such as dolls' legs. Pinch a small amount of filler at a time to prevent it from bunching up into a solid ball.

⊕ If I'm using buttons for eyes or anything that my grandchildren may want to play with, I pop a little wet fabric glue behind the button to help secure it.

⊕ If I'm tightly stuffing a project like a pincushion, I'll shorten my stitch length to make the seam strong. This means that there's less chance of the stitches bursting.

⊕ Choose a seam that won't be noticed to leave the gap for turning.

⊕ To hide the ends of your thread after hand sewing eyes or embellishments onto your finished project, push the needle into another area of the item and pull tight. Snip off the thread and when you let go, the end of the thread will pop inside.

⊕ I live in an old stone bakery which can be quite draughty, so draught excluders in my doorways are essential. I fill them with rolled-up towels to help absorb moisture from freshly cleaned floors or rainy wet days!

⊕ Add a zip to the base of a doorstop. You'll be able to change the stuffing if it gets damp, and it makes a perfect hiding place for spare keys!

⊕ To help turn thin tubes, thread a long, quite blunt embroidery needle with strong thread, knot the end, and take it through the end of the tube. Feed the needle through the tube and the thread will pull the end of the tube through.

DIY TEMPLATES

I'm a major fan of templates – plastic shapes that you simply draw around to create anything from appliqué to full-sized bags. I prefer plastic or acrylic, transparent templates so that I can see through them for perfect placement. However, as we don't always have the perfect template for our projects to hand, here are a few household items I use that can do the trick.

CIRCLES

Probably the most versatile template shape – I use a circle to round off corners, make purse flaps, coasters and flowers. Embroidery hoops come in many sizes but be aware that they may not actually make the perfect circle. Explore your crockery cupboard for plates, saucers, bowls and egg cups to draw around, then raid your stash of ribbons – you'll probably find many sizes of circular spools!

The largest plate I have measures 30cm (12in) across, so if I need a larger circle I'll make a quarter circle template by pinning a tape measure to the corner of a sheet of card, then marking an arc to half the size of circle I need. I'll fold my fabric into four before transferring the mark and cutting.

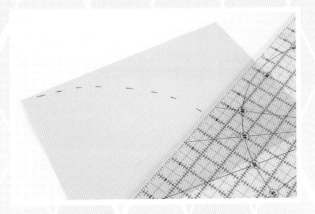

OVALS

There aren't many oval-shaped plates in my cupboard, so I make my own from circles. Draw two circles then join them together across the top and bottom. Presto!

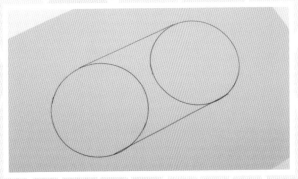

HEARTS

The perfect heart is difficult for most of us to draw, so here's a simple technique that you can use to create any shape of heart you'll need. Fold your template paper in half. Decide on the size of your heart and choose a circle template of about half the size. Place the circle over the fold and draw around it. Take a straight line from the edge of the circle to the fold. Cut out the shape and open to see the heart shape. Experiment with different sized circle templates, and lengthen the straight line to create a more modern style of heart.

STORAGE

For me, being organized in the sewing room is vital. I like to have my most used tools to hand and fabrics stored in order of colour. I have a drawer for felt, one for faux leathers and one for smaller pieces of fabric, while coloured cottons are kept in boxes on shelves in my store room. I appreciate that not everyone can give over their entire house to sewing, so storage space is precious!

Items that I need daily, or things that decorate and brighten up my room, are made as attractive as possible, but the plastic boxes for fabric and props are shut away in my store cupboard.

⊕ Simple shelving with baskets filled with zips and trimmings is a terrific way of using wall space.

⊕ Rolls of interfacing and stabilizers can be stored upright in baskets under your sewing table.

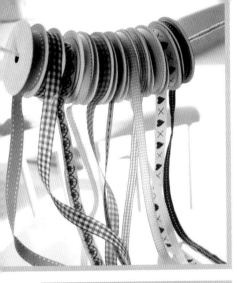

⊕ Cutlery trays make practical ribbon holders… or try stringing the ribbon reels onto cord and hanging them across a window.

⊕ Most of my threads are stored on racks on the wall… but it's fun to find unusual items like this mini supermarket basket to store bobbins and spools of thread.

⊕ Plant pots made from either terracotta or tin make good storage bins for marking tools, tweezers, glues and rulers.

⊕ A clever way to fill a corner of a room is to use a free-standing coat rack. I hang bags, embroidery hoops and occasionally a coat on mine…

⊕ A fabric-covered decorative mannequin could be used as a pin board for fabric and ribbon swatches.

⊕ Jam jars may be an obvious choice for buttons which look lovely on shelving, but I also keep elastic bungees, spare sewing machine feet, glue sticks and beads in old coffee jars – they're not so pretty, so are kept out of sight.

⊕ Don't overlook the potential storage space on the backs of doors – a perfect place to store your craft bag or scraps of fabric in home-made drawstring bags!

SEWING KNOW-HOW

MACHINE STITCHES

You may have two or two hundred stitches on your machine – utility stitches for project construction and decorative stitches for embellishment. Take a look in the manufacturer's manual to see the recommended presser feet to use with the different stitches. In most cases the feet are lettered and some machines will display the foot required on the screen. These are the stitches I use the most:

STRAIGHT STITCH

The most useful stitch on your machine! Use for joining fabric, gathering, top-stitching and tacking/basting. You should be able to alter the length of the stitch where necessary on your machine. On many machines, the stitch width function will swing the needle from left to right. By contrast, adjusting the length of the stitch doesn't affect the needle: it changes the rate at which the feed dogs draw the fabric through. A shorter stitch forms a strong seam and is preferable to use with fine fabrics. The majority of sewing machines will default to a 2.4 or 2.5mm stitch length – this is suitable for most fabrics. Long stitches are sewn with a looser tension and are easy to remove, making them an appropriate choice for tacking/basting. You may prefer the look of a longer stitch when top-stitching your project.

TRIPLE STRAIGHT STITCH

This is a stitch designed for stretch fabrics, as the backstitch technique has a little 'give', preventing the stitches from breaking when stretched. It creates a thick line of stitching forming a useful top-stitch on fabrics like denim.

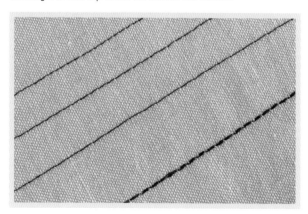

TOP-STITCHING

This is a straight stitch that is seen from the front of your project. An edge stitch is a straight stitch sewn close to the edge of your work.

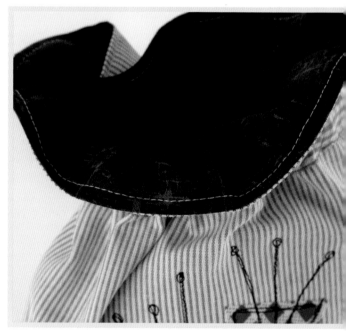

Short 1.5mm straight stitch is shown at the top, then standard 2.5mm straight stitch, then tacking 5mm, and at the bottom is triple straight stitch.

OVER-EDGE STITCH

This stitch works best with an over-edge foot (see page 19). The thread wraps around the edge of the fabric, finishing off seams and helping to prevent fraying. A great alternative to an overlocker/serger if you're not ready for that investment yet...

BUTTONHOLE STITCH

A buttonhole stitch is a short zigzag stitch, using a special presser foot on your machine (see page 18). You can choose assorted styles of hole depending on your project and your machine. I use a standard shape for pillow covers, bags and blouses. A keyhole works well with heavy fabrics and buttons with shanks, making it perfect for coats and jackets.

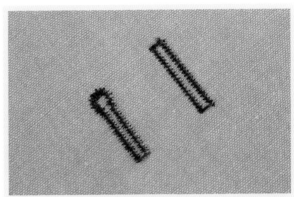

BLIND HEM STITCH

This stitch sews along the inside of your hem with a straight stitch, then occasionally throws a zigzag stitch into the fold of the hem, catching just a couple of threads to keep the stitches as invisible as possible from the right side of your project. Used for dressmaking and curtains, this is also a useful stitch for adding appliqué. A blind hem stitch foot is used (see page 19), which has an adjustable guide.

Blind hem stitch.

Blind hem stitch appliqué.

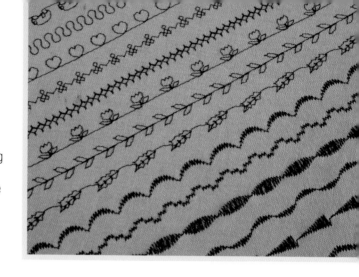

DECORATIVE STITCHES

Decorative stitches vary from machine to machine, and can be anything from flowers and leaves, to abstract stitching, children's motifs and the alphabet. Some computerized sewing machines will have a memory to store a selection of letters and stitch designs. My most used decorative stitch is a simple blanket stitch, I use this to edge fabric or add appliqué.

Satin stitches (bottom of picture opposite) are variations on the zigzag stitch so create a denser row of stitches.

ZIGZAG STITCH

Neatening seams, appliqué, sewing on buttons, darning, free-motion embroidery and decorative trims make the zigzag stitch a must-have on your sewing machine. The width can be altered – when the length of the stitch is shortened it forms a bold line, called a 'satin' stitch, which is used for appliqué.

TRIPLE ZIGZAG STITCH

This is your regular zigzag stitch, but with the needle sewing over the stitch three times to form a bold, decorative effect.

THREE-STEP ZIGZAG STITCH

Sometimes a wide zigzag stitch can cause the fabric to roll under the stitch, in which case use the three-step zigzag stitch which adds a couple of small stitches in between the points. Perfect for sewing in elastic. Stretch the elastic slightly as you sew, and set the width of the stitch as close to the width of the elastic as you can.

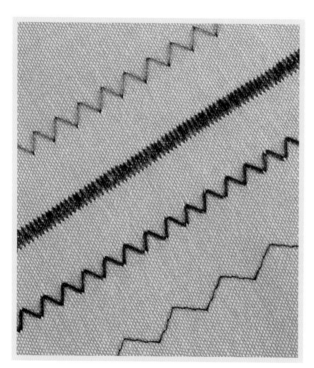

Zigzag at the top, then satin, triple and three-step.

MOCK HAND STITCH

This is a clever stitch that uses clear thread on the top of the machine, and coloured thread on the bottom. Increase the tension on the top of your machine to its maximum and the bottom thread will be pulled through to the top. The result is a row of alternative clear and coloured thread, giving the illusion of a hand-sewn running stitch! Perfect for quilters or to add a hand-made touch to bags, pockets, collars or even bed linen.

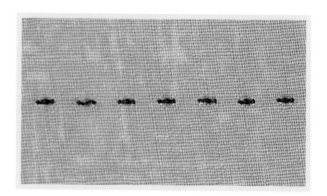

44

FAGOTING STITCH

This is a decorative stitch used to join two pieces of fabric on the fold, with a gap along the centre which looks effective with a contrasting fabric placed behind it.

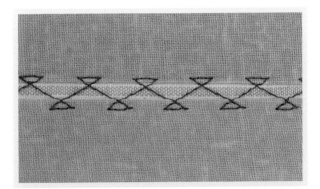

DARNING STITCH

Many machines will have a darning stitch. I've used red on blue here so that the stitches stand out, but if you use the same colour thread as your fabric you'll sew a thread 'patch' that can barely be seen.

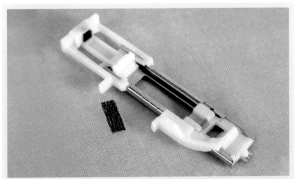

HAND STITCHES

Although much of your work will use the sewing machine, there are a few hand stitches you'll find useful, for invisibly sewing openings closed, or tacking/basting zips, for example.

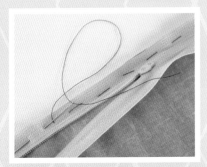

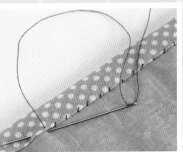

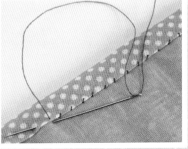

Tacking/basting stitch

A long running stitch used to temporarily hold fabrics together while sewing; the stitches are removed after the project is finished. I find it easier to tack/baste a zip in place rather than use pins, which can be difficult to sew around.

Slip stitch

Use this stitch along the fold of bias tape to secure. Take the needle into the base fabric, bring it up through the fold of the tape, then back directly underneath and repeat. I've used a contrasting colour of thread here so that you can see the stitch, but use the same colour as the bias binding for the most impressive results.

Ladder stitch

Used for bringing together two folded lengths of fabric, for instance when closing an opening in the lining of a bag, or closing a seam in a stuffed toy. Sew into the fold on one side with a small stitch, take the needle straight across the gap and into the opposite fold, sew into the fold again and repeat. After sewing a few stitches, gently pull the thread and the gap will close. Use the same colour thread as your fabric, or for the most invisible stitches on patterned fabric, choose a grey or beige thread.

SEAMS

SEAM ALLOWANCE

This is the distance from the raw edge of your fabric to the line of stitches. Read the instructions or pattern for your project as the seam allowance will vary; for patchwork it tends to be 5mm (¼in) and dressmakers generally use 1.5cm (⅝in). However, I recently started making up a man's shirt without reading the instructions and automatically used a 1.5cm (⅝in) seam allowance. I was halfway through the collar before I realized it should have been 5mm (¼in)… I now need to find a small boy for that shirt to fit!

For most of your seams, use the default straight stitch length on your computerized sewing machine which is usually 2.5 (this is mm); on mechanical machines you'll need to turn a knob to choose the right setting. Change the stitch to a shorter length if you're making projects that are stuffed, for instance toys or doorstops, as the smaller stitch will be stronger under stress. A shorter stitch may work well in finer fabric, but use a long stitch for tacking/basting or gathering. For decorative top-stitching the choice is yours. Test on a scrap piece of fabric first to make sure you're happy with the finished effect.

Altering the stitch length doesn't change the needle action, but the speed at which the feed dogs draw the fabric under the needle.

Read your pattern instructions to see if the designer recommends pressing the finished seams open or to one side. Quilters may prefer to press to the side particularly if they are stitching 'in the ditch' (sewing through the layers along the seams), while dressmakers usually press the seams open.

FINISHING SEAMS

I don't worry too much about finishing seams that won't be seen, for instance inside lined bags, but for dressmaking or homewares the neat, unfrayed edges give a more professional look. How you finish your seams is a matter of choice.

⊕ Use **pinking shears** to trim the raw edges for a quick way to stop fabric from fraying.

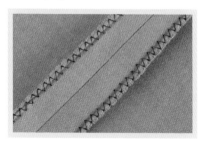

⊕ Alternatively, use the **zigzag stitch**.

⊕ An **overlocker/serger** is beneficial if you're sewing large projects like curtains, or if you intend to sell the items you make. These machines take the threads over the edge of the fabric, trimming the edge with a blade as you sew. However, if you don't want to go to the extra expense, many sewing machines will have an **over-edge stitch** that does a similar job.

⊕ To create a **clean edge finish** on your seam, neaten the raw edges by folding over once or twice and hemming. This is quite time-consuming and may create too much bulk on finer fabrics.

FRENCH SEAMS

This seam requires no finishing as the raw edges can't be seen – the seam looks the same on both the inside and outside of your work. Use this on fine or sheer fabric, pillowcases and unlined bags where a raw seam could look ugly. Use the same colour thread as your fabric.

1 Sew your fabrics wrong sides together. Trim the seam allowance to 3mm (⅛in).

2 Fold the fabric over the seam right sides together. Sew with a 5mm (¼in) seam allowance, trapping the raw edges in the centre. Open out and press.

3 You will have a neat seam with no raw edges showing from either side.

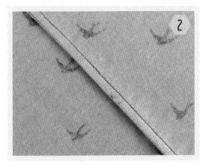

FLAT FELLED SEAMS

A flat felled seam is used to strengthen the seams on garments that tend to take a bit of stress, like the inside leg seam of jeans, or childrenswear. It makes a neat join, with no raw edges showing on either side of the garment. This seam can be sewn from either side of the fabric, but the most common way is to sew the fabric from the right side. Use either the same colour or a contrasting thread.

1 Sew a 1.5cm (⅝in) seam allowance with your fabric wrong sides together. Press the seam open. Trim away one side of the seam allowance, taking it to 5mm (¼in).

2 Fold the wider seam over the narrow seam allowance and press.

3 Tuck the raw edge of the wider seam allowance under the fold and press again, making sure the flap of fabric is the same width all the way along. Top-stitch close to the fold, trapping the raw edge inside the seam.

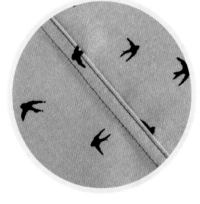

Flat felled seam viewed from the right side.

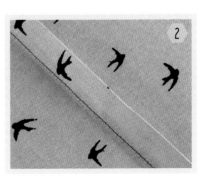

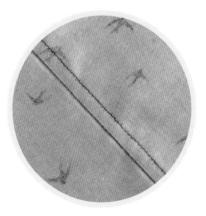

Flat felled seam viewed from the wrong side.

CUTTING

FUSSY CUTTING

This is a method of cutting a specific area of your fabric to centralize a pattern. Place a transparent ruler or template over the pattern you wish to cut out. Mark around the area with an erasable pen, then cut. You may want to use a specific part of a print for a flap or pocket on your bag, when having half the print just wouldn't look right!

CUTTING ACROSS CORNERS

This helps to keep the corners square when turned the right way out. Cut away the corner, keeping as close to the stitches as you can without snipping them.

TRIMMING CURVES

For curves that are to be turned, make little 'v'-shaped cuts into the fabric up to the seam – this will stop the fabric from puckering when turned. You could also use pinking shears for the same effect.

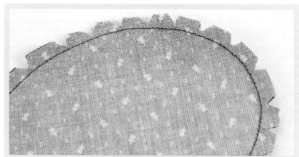

HOW TO GET THE BEST CUT

Cutting is an important part of sewing: the better your cutting, the better your sewing. If you have ever wondered how shears and scissors are different, then put simply, scissors have two handles of equal size and are symmetrical in shape, whereas shears have one handle larger than the other. Shears are bent to allow the blade to sit as flat as possible on your cutting surface. This allows for maximum control as you're cutting. You'll see that one of the blades is rounded – this prevents your fabric from snagging. Your thumb goes through the small handle, and all of your fingers should fit through the larger handle. Hold the shears firmly and upright when cutting, to achieve the best cut.

Scissors.

Metal handles help when cutting through thick fabrics, but it can be a little tiring on the hand. Plastic and comfort handled shears are also available. Serrated blades have a good grip, making them perfect for cutting sheer or slippery fabrics like silk.

Shears come in many different sizes. Try a 20–23cm (8–9in) blade if you're a beginner, or larger if you're more experienced at cutting and want to cut quickly or through thick fabrics.

Shears.

HEMS

Hems neaten the raw edges of your fabric. A cloth that doesn't fray doesn't need to be hemmed, for example, felt. For woven fabrics I'd suggest folding the edge over twice for a neat finish.

FOLDED HEM

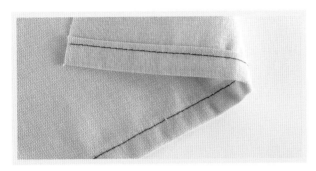

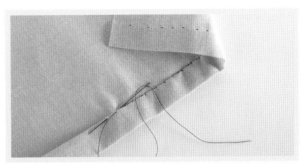

If you're machine sewing, fold your fabric over wrong sides together by about 12mm (½in) and press. Turn over again to the depth you require and press again. Sew along the first fold to hem. Use the same colour of thread as your fabric if you don't want the stitches to stand out, or you could use a contrasting colour thread to make a decorative border.

To hand sew, fold the fabric in the same way, and use a slip stitch in the same colour thread as your fabric. Take the needle through the folded fabric then catch just a couple of threads of the main fabric to keep the stitches as small as possible. (I've used a contrasting colour of thread so you can see the stitches clearly.)

BLIND HEM

The stitches on this hem should barely be seen. It takes a bit of practice so test on a scrap piece of the same fabric as your project first. I've used red thread on blue fabric so you can see the stitches, but when you sew your hems use the same colour as your project or clear thread to make them as invisible as possible.

1 Finish off the raw edge of your fabric either with an over-edge stitch or by folding the edge over by about 12mm (½in) and pressing.

2 Fold over again to the depth you require and press. The hem can be as deep as you like, depending on the project you're making.

3 Fold the hem over, right sides together, exposing the first fold but keeping the raw edge hidden. You'll sew along the first fold. Choose the blind hem stitch on your sewing machine. This will form a straight stitch along the edge of the fabric, with an occasional stitch that should catch the inside of the main fabric. Use the guide on your blind hem presser foot against the fabric fold.

4 Open out the seam and press.

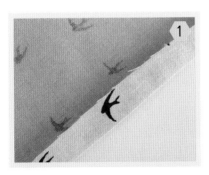

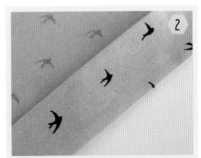

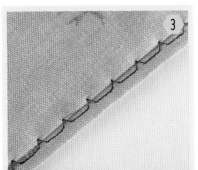

Project
HEART PINCUSHION

Techniques

- Making a template
- Snipping curves
- Cutting corners
- Ladder stitch

Notes

Use a 5mm (¼in) seam allowance

You will need

- DIY heart template measuring 15cm (6in) in length (see page 37)
- 30cm (12in) square of cotton fabric
- 30cm (12in) length of ribbon, 12mm (½in) wide
- Approx. 50g (2oz) toy filler

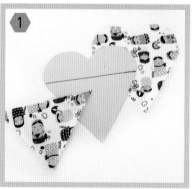

1 Cut out two heart shapes from cotton fabric. Draw a horizontal line across your template, 10cm (4in) up from the point, and cut out two identical triangular pieces.

2 Sew the two triangles right sides together across the top. Turn over and press, then top-stitch along the seam.

3 Place the triangle over the base of the right side of one piece of heart fabric, and sew along the right-hand side.

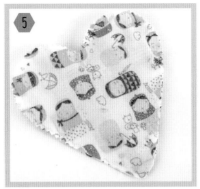

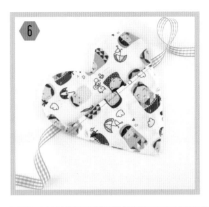

4 Sew the ribbon horizontally, central to the remaining heart fabric, 2.5cm (1in) down from the 'v' at the top of the heart shape.

5 Sew the two hearts right sides together, leaving a turning gap of about 5cm (2in) over the side section you previously sewed. Make sure you don't trap the ribbon in your seam! When you come to the 'v' shape, sew one stitch straight across instead of pivoting, this will make the point crisper when you turn the heart. Snip off the seam allowance at the point of the heart, cut around the curves with pinking shears, and cut into the 'v' shape at the top.

6 Turn the right side out. The ribbon should be on the opposite side to the pocket, and the opening at the side.

7 Stuff with toy filler, then sew the opening closed with a ladder stitch.

8 Flip the pocket over to the same side as the ribbon, pop your scissors into the pocket, thread the ribbon through the handles and tie in a bow. Trim the ends of the ribbon at an angle to stop fraying.

ZIPS

Who would have thought there were so many types of zips! I keep a box of different colours and lengths of zips as I use so many, for dressmaking, bags, purses and pillow covers. Below is what you'll find in my zip box.

TYPES OF ZIP

Continuous zipping
This is bought in lengths; sometimes the sliders are already attached, sometimes you need to attach them yourself. Extra sliders are usually available.

Nylon zips
The most common type of zip and the one I use most often, for dressmaking, craft and homewares. The coil is a continuous chain as opposed to 'teeth' – if pulled, you'd have one long piece of nylon wire! I choose a zip that is longer than I need which means I can sew with the slider out of the way, and it can be cut to size so I don't have to worry about buying the exact length of zip I need.

Nylon zips with transparent tape
Perfect for lightweight fabric and dressmaking, or for a fabric colour that's difficult to match.

Metal-tooth zips
These are strong zips, that are good for outerwear and jeans. They have individual metal teeth that are fixed evenly along the tape.

Open-ended zips
Metal or plastic teeth are fixed along the zip tape. The two sides of the zip come apart completely, making the zip perfect for coats, jackets and sleeping bags.

Decorative zips
The lacy zip tape is meant to be seen, so the zip is sewn to the top of projects such as cosmetic bags and purses.

Invisible zips
Usually used for dressmaking, the zip shouldn't be seen when fitted, apart from the teardrop-shaped zip pull.

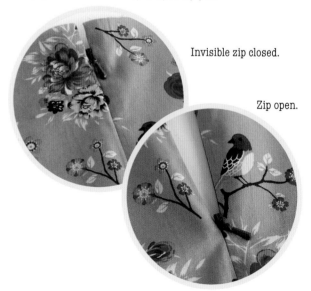

Invisible zip closed.

Zip open.

52

PARTS OF A ZIP

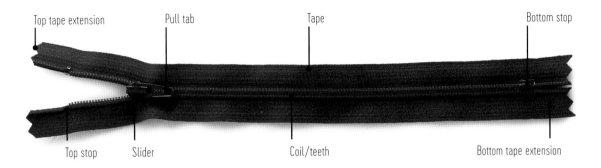

Top tape extension · Pull tab · Tape · Bottom stop

Top stop · Slider · Coil/teeth · Bottom tape extension

ZIP TIPS

⊕ I like to buy zips longer than I need, then trim them to size after sewing. This doesn't work on 100 per cent of projects, but it's a handy trick to use where you can, as the slider can be pushed out of the way while sewing, helping to keep the stitch line straight. Nylon zips can be easily trimmed, but be careful if you cut the stopper from the ends of the zip that the slider doesn't come off! Don't try to cut a zip with metal teeth or you'll ruin your scissors.

⊕ Zips on a roll are a cost-effective option; you can simply cut off any length you like (see right). If you need to add a slider, snip along the tape on the left-hand side of the zip, alongside the coil, then off at a diagonal. Cut the tape on the opposite side straight across, through the coil. Push the slider onto the exposed coil, and when you meet the opposite side of the zip, gently push this into the opposite side of the slider. This doesn't always work first time, so persevere.

⊕ To lubricate a zip and help it run smoothly try rubbing lip balm, candle wax, soap or a graphite pencil over the teeth. Wipe off any residue.

⊕ If you're turning through a bag or pillow cover, remember to open the zip before the final construction stages as you'll need to pull the fabric through the opening.

⊕ When approaching the slider as you're sewing in a zip, leave the needle in the down position and manoeuvre the slider out of the way. This will help to keep your stitch line straight.

⊕ You may find it easier to use a temporary glue as opposed to tacking/basting your zip by hand, before sewing (see middle right).

⊕ If you're sewing a zip into a pillow cover, cosmetic bag or a letterbox style of opening, sew the open ends of the zip together first and you'll find it easier to sew (see right).

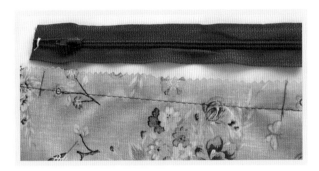

Zips on a roll can be cut to any size.

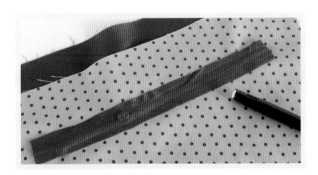

Use a temporary glue before sewing.

Sew the open ends of the zip together.

LETTERBOX ZIP

I call this a 'letterbox' zip as the opening reminds me of a letterbox and the lining fabric is 'posted' through the hole. I use it to create pockets in bag linings. I prefer to use nylon continuous zips for this as they can be cut to size.

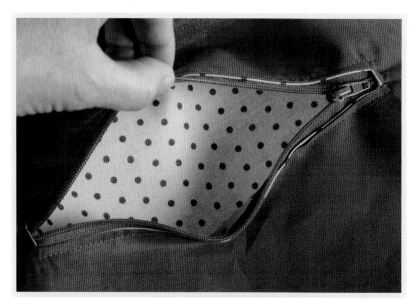

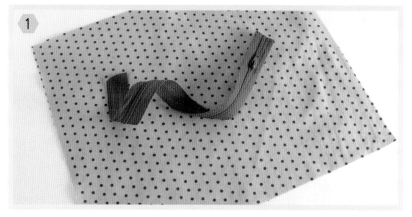

1 Cut two pieces of lining fabric to the size of the pocket you need. This should be shorter than your bag lining fabric, and can either be the same width so that the pocket is sewn into the side seam, or narrower than the bag. Choose a zip that is about 5cm (2in) longer than the pocket opening; it will sit flatter when the ends (with the metal stoppers) are cut off.

2 Draw a rectangle onto the wrong side of one lining piece in the position you'd like the zip, measuring 12mm (½in) wide, and the length of the zip opening. Draw a horizontal line straight through the centre of the rectangle, with a 'y' shape at each end going into the corners of the rectangle.

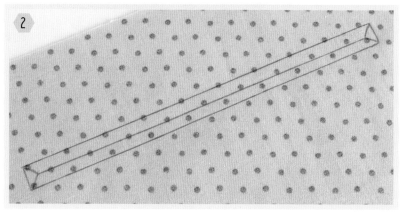

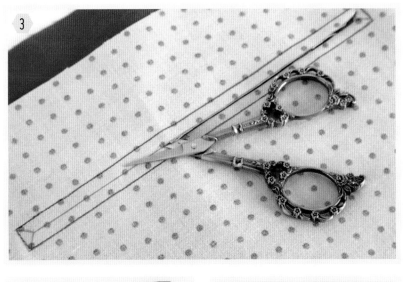

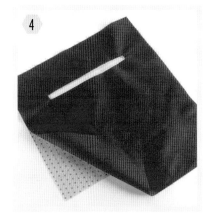

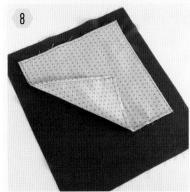

3 Pin right sides together to your bag lining fabric. With a small stitch on your machine, carefully sew around the rectangle you have drawn. Take a small sharp pair of scissors and cut along the centre line, then into the 'y' shape, up to (but not through) the stitches. Remove the pins.

4 Push the lining through the hole, and press.

5 Place the zip behind the hole. Either tack/baste or use temporary glue to hold the zip in place, then sew on your machine.

6 Pin the two pocket pieces right sides together keeping the bag lining out of the way. If your pocket is going to fit into the side seam, sew across the top and bottom of the pocket.

7 Tack/baste the pocket to the side of the lining. Remove the pins.

8 If your pocket is narrower than the width of the lining, sew all around the two pocket pieces avoiding sewing through the lining fabric.

INVISIBLE ZIPS

Invisible or concealed zips should be just that: unseen. When you look at the zip, the coil is on the wrong side, and the slider usually has a teardrop-shaped pull. These are usually fitted in dresses and skirts, and I occasionally like to use an invisible zip in the seams of pillow covers. See page 52 for an open and closed invisible zip.

Although you can fit an invisible zip with a standard zipper foot, it's well worth investing in an invisible zipper foot, to make the job a lot quicker! They will look slightly different depending on the make of your machine, but all will have two grooves which help to open out the coil of the zip when sewing.

Invisible zipper feet.

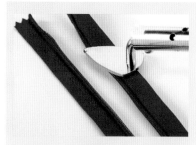

Tip

Before sewing, open the zip and uncurl the coiled edges. Press lightly with a small iron or a bamboo creaser.

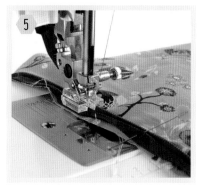

1 With this type of zip, you'll sew the seam after the zip has been inserted. To make it a bit easier, place the zip in between the two fabric pieces.

2 Fold the zip over the left-hand piece of fabric, edges together, with the zip 5mm (¼in) from the top, and pin it in place.

3 Place the left-hand groove of the zipper foot over the coil and sew. The stitches should sit just underneath the coil.

4 Place the remaining side to the second piece of fabric, and pin.

5 Put the coil under the right-hand groove of the zipper foot and sew.

6 Now the zip will be stitched but the seam underneath is open.

7 Fold the fabric in half right sides together, and sew the seam up to the point where your seam stitches meet the zip stitches, moving the end of the zip out of the way as you sew.

LAP ZIP

This type of closure is used in dressmaking, particularly skirts. The wider side of the seam slightly overlaps the smaller, so that the zip is covered when closed.

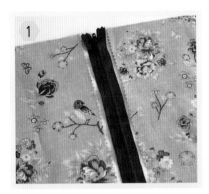

1 Mark the length of your zip on your fabric, just above the bottom stopper.

2 Sew the seam up to this point. Press the seam open.

3 Turn the fabric over to the right side. Gently roll the left-hand side of the pressed seam back by 3mm (⅛in) and pin this edge to the side of the zip coil. This is what makes the fabric overlap.

4 With the zipper foot on your machine, sew along this edge. You'll need to move the slider out of the way as you sew.

5 When you close the zip you'll see how the fabric overlaps.

6 Pin the second side of the fabric to the remaining zip tape and sew, straight across the bottom of the zip and back alongside the coil to the top. Then press.

This is the finished zip closed.

This is the finished zip open.

PILLOW COVER ZIP

This is the easiest way to fit a zip into the middle of a seam, making it perfect for pillow covers. Use a nylon zip for best results.

1 Take your two pieces of fabric and place them right sides together. Place the zip next to the seam, and mark on your fabric 12mm (½in) from the top and bottom, or just inside the top and bottom stoppers. Sew from the edge of your fabric to the first mark and reverse a couple of stitches, then increase the length of stitch to its maximum and sew to the next mark. Backstitch. Readjust your stitch to the regular length and sew to the end of your fabric.

2 Press the seam open. Place your zip face down over the centre of the seam and pin, then tack/baste all the way round (use a glue stick if you prefer). Remove the pins.

3 Put the zipper foot on your machine and sew all the way around the zip. Turn over your work, and using your seam ripper, carefully cut through the long stitches over the zip coil. Remove the tacking/basting stitches and you're finished.

PIPING

A strip of piping around a bag gives a professional finishing touch to your work, and is simple to make yourself. Cord comes in many different sizes, but for pillow cover or bag seams I'd use cord up to 5mm (¼in) wide.

1 Cut your fabric into strips, wide enough to wrap around the cord plus a good 5mm (¼in) to go under the sewing machine needle. If you're taking the piping around curves and corners, then cut the fabric strips on the bias. Pin the raw edges together, sandwiching the cord in the centre.

2 Using the zipper foot on your machine, sew alongside the cord, making sure the raw edges are together. Take out the pins as you sew.

3 If necessary, trim the flat section of the fabric to the width of your seam allowance. You may want to invest in a piping gauge to achieve the perfect width.

4 To apply the piping to your fabric, sandwich it in between the two pieces of fabric, right sides and raw edges together, then sew with your zipper foot. (Piping feet are available for some sewing machines.) As a new sewer, you may find it easier to sew the piping to one side of your work at a time. Keep your needle close to the cord without actually sewing through it.

5 To join piping around projects such as pillow covers, trim the piping cord inside the fabric by about 2.5cm (1in). Fold the fabric inwards by 12mm (½in), sew the piping cord raw edges together to the right side of the fabric.

6 Apply the binding around the fabric, then when it meets, tuck the end of the cord inside the fold of the first end.

7 Sew straight across the join. It should be barely visible when the piping is turned over.

8 If you're taking your piping around a corner, sew up to 5cm (2in) away from the corner and stop, then make a couple of snips into the piping cord seam allowance to enable it to bend. The corners will always be slightly rounded, but this technique makes them as square as possible.

9 For curves, make a few snips into the seam allowance around the piping cord before sewing to your fabric.

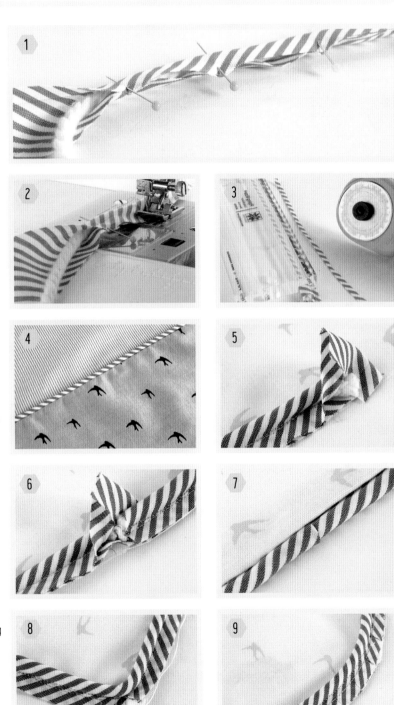

Project
PILLOW COVER

1 Place the two rectangular pieces of fabric right sides together. Mark 5cm (2in) from the top and bottom of one long edge – this will be the opening for the zip. (I like to choose a long zip and cut it to size, this way I don't have the metal stoppers in my project.) Sew with a stitch length of 2.5 with a 12mm (½in) seam allowance, from the top of the fabric to your first mark. Backstitch a couple of stitches. Elongate your stitch to the longest on your machine and sew to the second mark. Backstitch again, take your stitch length back to 2.5 and continue sewing.

2 Press the seam open.

3 Cut either end off your zip to make it 30cm (12in) in length. Hand sew the open ends together, to make it easier to insert. Place the zip face down over the seam and tack/baste in place.

4 With the zipper foot on your sewing machine, sew around the zip in a box shape. Carefully unpick the stitches over the zip using your quick unpick.

5 Wrap your bias strip of fabric around the cord to create piping as shown on page 59, then sew the piping around the edge of the square piece of fabric, snip into the corners and overlap the join.

6 Sew the zipped section right sides together to the piped piece, making sure the zip is open. Turn the right side out and press. If you turn the pillow cover and the stitching around the corners doesn't look neat, turn it back again and re-sew.

7 Push the pillow pad inside your cover.

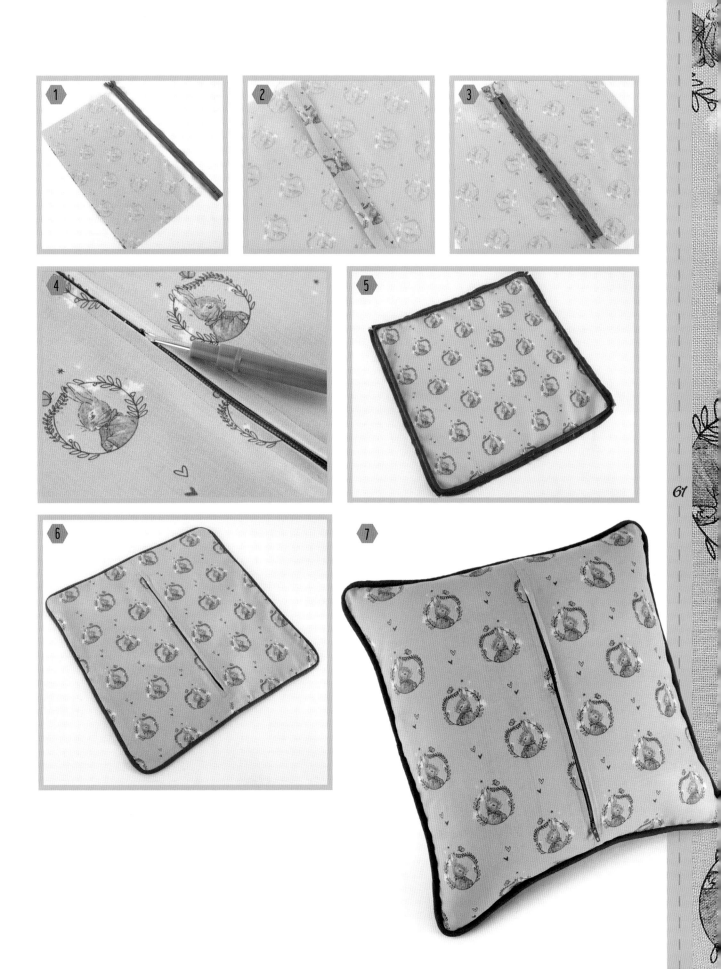

SHIRRING

Shirring is a method of sewing with fine elastic thread in the bobbin of your sewing machine. As you sew in rows of straight lines, the fabric becomes ruched and stretchy. This is a simple, quick way of making summer dresses or gathering waists, wrists and necklines when dressmaking. The colours of thread available are quite limited, but the elastic is only seen on the wrong side of the fabric so don't worry about finding a perfect colour match.

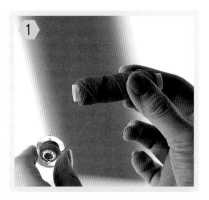

62

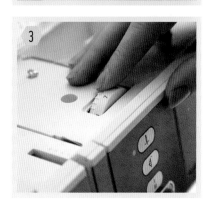

1 The elastic thread only goes in the bobbin, and you'll need to wind it by hand to avoid stretching. If you're shirring a large area you'll have to refill a few times, but it's worth it.

2 Pop the bobbin into its casing, as you would with ordinary thread. Whether you have a front- or top-loading bobbin, make sure you take the elastic thread through the tensions. Use regular thread in the top of your machine.

3 Increase the stitch length so that it's slightly longer than you'd normally use, and try sewing on a scrap piece of the same fabric you're using. The elastic should be quite tight, but not pulled through to the top of your fabric. Different machines behave in different ways, and you may need to adjust the tension slightly to get the perfect stitch. Practise on a piece of scrap fabric first.

4 Before shirring your garment fabric, hem or overlock the raw edge first, as you'll find this difficult to do after the fabric has gathered. Sew the first line of stitches with elastic thread and you'll see the fabric gathering up. Leave about 7.5cm (3in) of thread at either end of your work so that you can tie it off to secure. Sew the second row of stitches 12mm (½in) from the first, and gently pull the fabric straight as you sew.

5 Keep sewing in this way until the area you need is gathered. Knot the ends of the threads and trim. To tighten the elastic, steam over the fabric with an iron and the elastic will shrink slightly.

FREE-MOTION EMBROIDERY

I really enjoy this embroidery technique, to add texture to quilting projects, to attach appliqué shapes, to get creative with stitching artwork, but most of all, to have fun! Here's how it works.

⊕ Think of your needle and thread as a pen and ink, but instead of moving the pen over the paper, you move the fabric under the needle to create your own unique designs. You will need a drop feed dog facility for your sewing machine (the feed dogs are the teeth that carry the fabric through the machine; by dropping these out of the way, you have control over moving the fabric in any direction you like) or a darning plate to cover the feed dogs, making them inactive. You'll also need a free-motion or darning foot. This foot 'hops' across the fabric, and allows you to see where you're stitching. It's also a good idea to practise on a piece of fabric you're not too precious about!

⊕ Use iron-on or tear-away stabilizer on the back of your fabric to give it substance and stop it from twisting, particularly on stretch fabrics like jersey knit. You can use a hoop if you wish, but you may find it a hindrance on larger designs.

⊕ So, put the feed dogs down and your machine foot on. Pop your fabric under the needle, your foot on the pedal and start to sew. Lay your hands flat either side of the needle, and move from side to side, up and down, around in circles, swirls, zigzags, any way you wish but just keep moving! It's good practice to stop after the first few stitches, leaving the needle down, and snip off the excess thread so you don't sew over it. You'll realize as you sew that the faster you move the fabric, the longer the stitch. There are no rules; stitch at a speed you feel comfortable with and like the look of. Quilters' gloves can help your fingers to grip the fabric, and keep your embroidery area clean.

⊕ When you've had a practice, take your work out of your machine and turn it over. You may find that the tension on some machines needs tightening, but check your manual for tension recommendations.

⊕ Try cutting fabric shapes, and doodling the appliqué in place. I like the 'sketchy' look of going over the outline a few times, and it really doesn't matter if your lines aren't straight.

⊕ You may not think of yourself as an artist, but we're all capable of abstract scribblings that look wonderful when doodled in beautifully coloured threads! Use an erasable ink pen to draw your design before stitching, or try scanning in a drawing to your computer, maybe some of your children's artwork, and printing it onto printable fabric and embroidering over the top.

⊕ Free-motion embroidery has a significant place in the quilting world; you'll see stippling and texture in many distinctive designs, not just to add interest to the project but to hold the layers of fabric and wadding together. The stitches can meander in a puzzle-like manner all over the quilt, or in designs like feathers and pebbles which are a little more advanced. As a beginner, have fun just doodling… There's no right or wrong, and you don't need specialist sewing skills to achieve beautiful and original designs.

Try outlining appliqué shapes – the stitching around these birds gives the impression of movement.

This is a photograph of one of my dogs, Alfie, printed onto canvas and then embroidered. I tried to pick out threads in colours to match his fur.

Project
SHIRRING DRESS

Techniques

- Shirring elastic
- French seam
- Hemming
- Button placement
- Appliqué

You will need

Measure the length of the dress you require, then add 5cm (2in). Measure around the child's chest and multiply this by two for the width. This is the size of the fabric you'll need. Mine measures 112×53cm (44×21in) and is for a two-year-old.

- Shirring elastic
- Four decorative buttons
- Four lengths of ribbon, each measuring 35.5cm (14in) in length and 2.5cm (1in) in width
- 15cm (6in) square of plain fabric for the appliqué

1 Create the appliqué shape. I copied by hand one of the rabbit shapes from my fabric, but if you're not too confident in hand drawing, try scanning the fabric then enlarging the shape on your computer. Alternatively, you could trace a shape from a picture. Position the shape to one side of the centre of the fabric, 7.5cm (3in) from the bottom, then sew (see page 70).

2 Sew the two sides of the fabric together with a French seam (see page 47), to make a tube.

3 Make a folded hem around the top and bottom (see page 49).

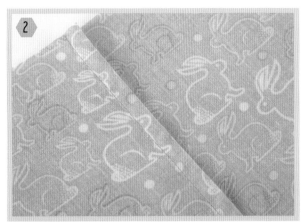

4 Load the shirring elastic into the bottom bobbin of your machine (see page 62), adjust the tension then begin to sew from the seam, all around the dress in a spiral, until you've covered approximately 10cm (4in) (or more on a larger dress).

5 If you can, try the dress on the child at this point, and mark the best position for the ribbon straps, with the seam at the back, two ribbons at the front and two at the back. Pin and sew the ribbons in place on the inside of the dress, then add decorative buttons to the front of the dress as shown. Tie the ribbons, trimming if necessary, then cut the ends at an angle to prevent fraying, and your dress is ready to wear.

BIAS BINDING

I use quite a lot of bias binding in my projects as it's a simple solution to finishing off raw edges and gives a professional finish to my work. Although it can be bought in many colours and sizes, I like to make my own as it's not only cost-effective, it also means I can co-ordinate my fabrics.

'Bias tape' is a strip of fabric cut on the diagonal, at a 45° angle, which allows a little 'give' so the fabric stretches around curves without puckering.

To cut your fabric accurately you'll need a rotary cutter, rectangular ruler and cutting mat (see page 25). Lay your fabric squarely on the cutting mat, place your ruler along the 45° mark on the mat, then cut.

CUTTING BIAS BINDING

1 Turn your fabric over, and use the straight side of the ruler to measure the width you need. For 2.5cm (1in) tape you'll need to cut 5cm (2in) of fabric.

2 As you cut across the triangle fabric, the length of the strips will increase, so fold the fabric in half matching up the diagonal edges and cut through two, three or four layers at a time.

3 To join the strips together, lay two pieces right sides together, overlapping at right angles. Draw a diagonal line from one corner to the other. Pin, then sew across this line. Trim the raw edge back to around 3mm (⅛in) and press the seam open.

4 Bias binding involves folding over both of the long edges of the tape into the centre and pressing. The easiest way to do this is to use either a bias binding machine or a small bias tape maker through which you thread the tape; it folds the strip in two and you press with your iron while pulling the fabric through. If you don't have a tape maker, carefully fold both long edges to the centre of the fabric strips and press. Be careful not to get your fingers too close to the iron!

SEWING BIAS BINDING

1 To apply the binding, first open up the crease lines. Right sides together, pin along the raw edge of your work. Sew with your machine along the crease mark.

2 Now fold the tape over the raw edge, and use a slip stitch to sew by hand.

Tip

If you're applying the bias tape all the way around a pillow cover so the ends meet, first fold over the end of the tape, open up the creases, pin and machine sew. Overlap the end of the tape by about 5mm (¼in). Fold over and stitch as above, or instead of slip stitching by hand you could machine top-stitch.

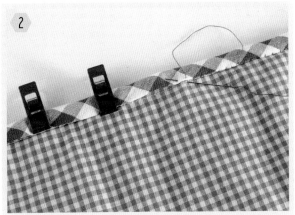

MITRING A CORNER

If the bias is attached around a curve it will stretch easily, but if you want to mitre a corner, follow the instructions below.

1 Sew again along the crease line but stop 5mm (¼in) from the corner and back-tack to stop the stitches from coming undone. Fold the tape along the second side, making a triangular pleat in the corner. Fold the pleat away from your stitch line, and sew straight down the second side.

2 Open up the tape at the corner and you should see a neat mitre forming. As you fold the tape over, mirror the same mitre on the reverse.

Mitre from the front.

Mitre from the back.

Project
TOASTER COVER

Techniques

- Making templates
- Bias binding
- Free-motion embroidery

Notes

Use a 5mm (¼in) seam allowance

You will need

To fit a 23 × 18 × 12.5cm (9 × 7 × 5in) toaster:

- 71 × 41cm (28 × 16in) outer fabric
- 71 × 41cm (28 × 16in) lining fabric
- 71 × 41cm (28 × 16in) wadding/batting (thermal wadding would make a good choice)
- 193cm (76in) of bias binding, 2cm (¾in) wide
- Free-motion embroidery foot
- Handful of toy filler
- 7.5cm (3in) circle template (see page 37)
- 10cm (4in) heart template (see page 37)
- Repositionable spray fabric adhesive
- Erasable marker pen

1 Measure the width, height and depth of your toaster. Mine is 23cm (9in) across, 18cm (7in) tall and 12.5cm (5in) deep.

2 Cut two lining pieces measuring 2.5cm (1in) larger on all sides, so mine measures 25.5cm (10in) across, by 20.5cm (8in) tall. For the top and side panel, cut a strip of fabric 2.5cm (1in) wider than your toaster (mine is therefore 15cm (6in) wide) to go around the top and sides of the cover. For the length, add the lining width to twice the lining height, i.e. 25.5 + 20.5 + 20.5cm (10 + 8 + 8in). This long strip will need trimming slightly later on.

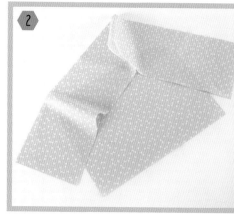

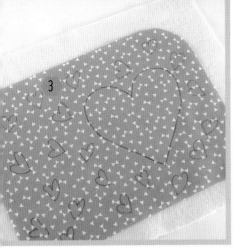

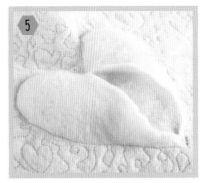

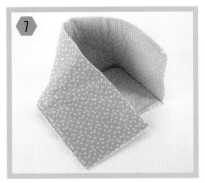

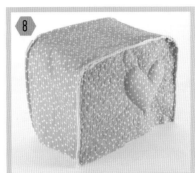

3 Use your circle template to curve the top corners of the front and back lining panels. Now, cut one long piece and a back piece from outer fabric to the same size and shape as the lining, then cut the front piece about 12mm (½in) larger all round. This piece will be quilted, which may 'shrink' the fabric slightly. Cut a piece of batting/wadding slightly larger than the front panel. Place the front panel over the wadding/batting and use a little spray adhesive to secure. Draw around your heart template, then draw a scattering of hearts all over the fabric.

4 With the free-motion embroidery foot on your machine, sew the outline of the large heart (see page 63). Then sew squiggly lines all over the fabric, joining up the small heart shapes as you sew, avoiding sewing inside the large heart.

5 Turn your work over and snip through the wadding/batting on the back of the large heart. Push a little toy filler inside.

6 Hand sew the opening closed – these stitches won't be seen so don't worry about neatness! Your heart will now be nicely plump. Trim the batting/wadding.

7 Place the embroidered panel over the back panel and trim to the same size if necessary. Place the front outer piece and lining piece right sides together, using spray adhesive to secure. Repeat with the back panels and the long top and side pieces. With lining pieces facing, sew the top panel to the front panel within the seam allowance. You'll now see that the top panel will be slightly longer.

8 Repeat with the opposite side. Trim the long panel to the same length as the front and back.

9 Apply bias binding around the sides, then around the bottom of the cover (see page 67). This project could easily be adapted for a sewing machine or food mixer cover.

APPLIQUÉ

Appliqué is the method of applying a decorative fabric motif to your work. This could be a hand-stitched felt shape, patterns cut from pre-printed fabric, fabric shapes you have drawn free hand, or using templates. There are many appliqué techniques varying in complexity, but for beginners, let's keep it simple.

Bear in mind you'll be sewing around the edge of your shape so don't choose a design that is too intricate – the outline of a hexagon is easier to sew than a tree!

To make the application a bit easier, use a repositionable spray adhesive to keep the shapes in place, or iron a sheet of fusible adhesive to the back of the fabric before cutting, then peel off the paper backing and re-iron the designs into position.

1 Draw or trace your motif onto the wrong side of your fabric. If you're using adhesive sheets, fuse to the wrong side of your fabric, then draw onto the paper backing. Remember that the image will be reversed.

2 Cut out your shape and place in position for sewing. Peel away the backing and press with your iron if you're using adhesive sheets; adhere with spray glue or hand tack/baste if you prefer. If you have trouble removing the paper backing from adhesive sheets, gently scratch the paper with a pin, then lift from the centre.

3 If you're machine sewing, form a dense line by shortening your zigzag stitch (satin stitch). This will also help woven fabrics from fraying. A fine thread will work best, choose 60wt for a good result, and make sure you have a sharp needle in your machine. Set your machine to 'needle down' if you have that function, otherwise make sure that if you lift the presser foot to turn the appliqué, you turn the hand wheel to put the needle in the down position.

Tip

If you need to trim fabric back to your stitches, appliqué (or duck-billed) scissors prevent the blade from cutting through the threads.

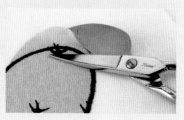

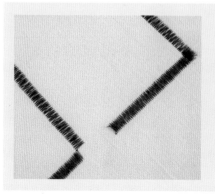

Tip

As a general rule, keep the needle to the right when pivoting; only move it over to the left if it's an inside curve or corner. The corner in the left of the image was turned with the needle in the down left position. The corner in the right of the image was turned with the needle in the down right position.

APPLIQUÉ EXAMPLES

I like the look of the simple blanket stitch – it gives a hand-sewn look to your work.

Try also using a blind hem stitch if you don't want to see so much of the stitch. Always test out the stitch you'd like to use on scrap fabric to make sure you're happy with the look before sewing your project.

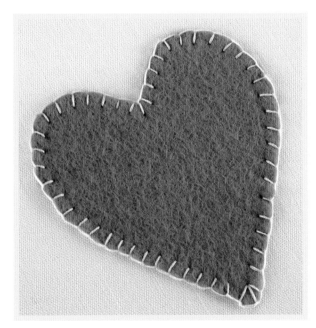

Felt appliqué looks charming when hand embroidered with a blanket or running stitch. The depth and texture of felt really makes the stitches stand out. Try hand stitching a blanket stitch around woven fabrics too – this gives a rustic look to your work.

Free-motion embroidery creates a charming hand-drawn finish, I particularly like to see the edges of the appliqué fraying slightly.

Project
DRAWSTRING BAG

1 Cut a 2cm (¾in) square from the bottom two corners of the lining and outer fabrics.

2 Iron the scraps of fabric to the adhesive sheet. Using your circle templates, cut three circles in each size, cut two of the large circles in half. For the leaves, cut rectangles of green fabric measuring 10 × 2.5cm (4 × 1in), then cut in half diagonally.

3 Arrange your design on the right side of one outer fabric piece, avoiding the top 7.5cm (3in) of fabric where your ribbon channel will be placed.

4 When you're happy with your design (you may not need to use all the fabric pieces), peel away the paper backing and iron in place. If any of your pieces overlap, just iron the bottom pieces for now; your design will look better if you sew the layers individually. Draw any stems and petals with your erasable marker if you wish, then for the fun bit, free-motion embroider over the lines.

5 Add any more layers of fabric and sew in place.

6 Fold the ends of each piece of ribbon under by 12mm (½in). Pin to the right side of the outer fabric pieces, centrally, 5cm (2in) from the top. Sew along either side of the ribbon, close to the edge, leaving the short ends open to create channels. Make sure you backstitch at the start and end of each line of stitching to strengthen the seam.

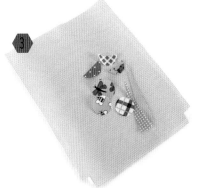

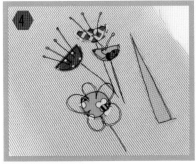

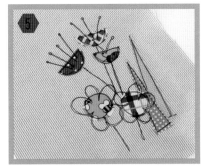

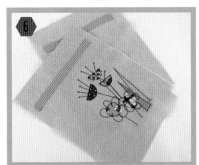

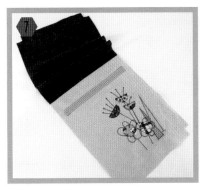

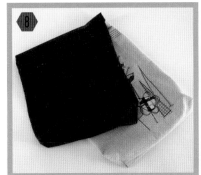

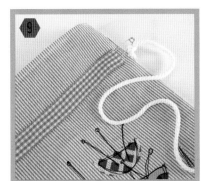

7 Sew the tops of the lining pieces right sides together to the top of the outer pieces. Press the seams towards the outer fabric.

8 Place the two sections right sides together and sew all the way round, leaving a turning gap of about 10cm (4in) in the bottom of the lining; don't sew the cut-out corners. Pull the corners open so that the side seams sit over the base seams and sew to make the base square. Turn the right side out and sew the opening closed with a ladder stitch.

9 Push the lining inside the bag and press, then edge stitch around the top of the bag. Knot one end of the cord and attach the safety pin, then thread the cord through both ribbon channels.

10 Knot the ends of the cord together and pull to close the bag.

BAG MAKING

Bags are top of the list of my favourite things to make. I enjoy working out how to construct innovative designs of bags and purses that aren't just attractive but practical too! Handbags always benefit from metal hardware to give them a shop-bought look, but many of these fastenings and furnishings don't come with instructions, so here's a few pointers.

FITTING EYELETS

Eyelets come in different sizes and colours, and are useful for threading drawstrings or decorative ribbon. Some eyelets can be fitted with a specialist tool. This is how to fit one of the most commonly used eyelet systems (but do always read the manufacturer's instructions as well).

1 Mark where you'd like your eyelet to go. With a small hammer, hit the cutting end of the tool supplied to make a hole.

2 Push the front, larger side of the eyelet from the front through to the back of the fabric.

3 Pop the second half of the eyelet that just looks like a ring, over the top.

4 Turn the tool around, place inside the ring, and hammer. This will squash the front of the eyelet around the back, to secure.

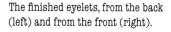

The finished eyelets, from the back (left) and from the front (right).

FITTING SNAP FASTENERS

Always follow the manufacturer's instructions with the snap fastener kits that you buy, but if you're a little confused, this is how the basic kits work.

You'll have a tool with a hole in one end, to cut the hole in your fabric. You'll also have a tool with a pointed end which you'll use to fix two pieces together.

The fasteners are in four pieces: two that clip together, then the front and back pieces.

1 Make sure you're working on a solid base; most kits will provide a hard disc to hammer into. Make a mark on your fabric where you want the fastener to go. Place the hole end of the small tool over the mark, and tap with a small hammer until you go through the fabric.

2 Push the 'stalk' of the domed side of the fastener through the hole.

3 Turn over, and place the shallow side of the inside of the fastener over the 'stalk'. The pointed tool goes into this stalk, and again, tap with the hammer. The stalk will split, curling over the sides to attach both sides together. Hammer until the fastener feels secure.

4 Repeat with the opposite sides of your fastener.

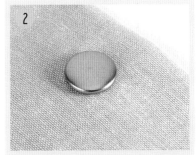

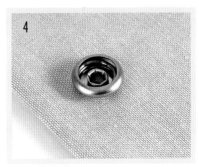

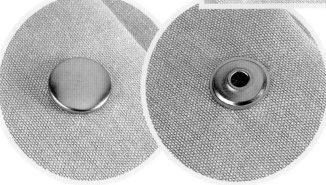

Left: This is how the fastener should look from the front when closed.

Right: This is how the fastener should look from the back.

FITTING MAGNETIC SNAPS

These easy-to-fit snaps don't usually come with instructions, so this is how to fit them. I'd recommend placing a scrap of fabric behind the snap, on the wrong side of your fabric, to stabilize the fabric and help to stop the snaps pulling. If you're fitting to a bag with a flap, the narrower side of the snap will go onto the flap and the wider section onto the bag.

The snaps come in two halves with a disc-shaped back section for each side.

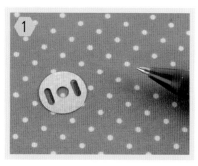
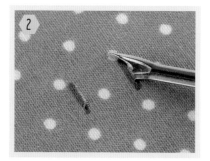
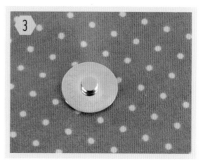

1 Mark the position of the snap with an erasable ink pen, placing the back of the snap on your fabric and drawing through the hole in the centre. Then mark the two long holes either side.

2 Take your seam ripper or a small pair of sharp scissors and make a small incision over the long lines. It's better to make the cuts too small so they can be made bigger. If you cut them too big you may ruin your project.

3 Push the prongs of the snaps through the holes.

4 Open out the prongs on the back of the fabric. It doesn't really matter whether you open them outwards or close them inwards. Personally I find them easier to open outwards.

FITTING LOCKS

Locks are well worth the time and effort to fit to your bag. They add a touch of elegance, a look of expense and of course they close your bag as well. These fastenings have several components – the clip or twist lock in two parts, backings and small screws. You'll also need a small screwdriver (try using the end of your tweezers if you don't have a screwdriver) and a small, sharp pair of scissors.

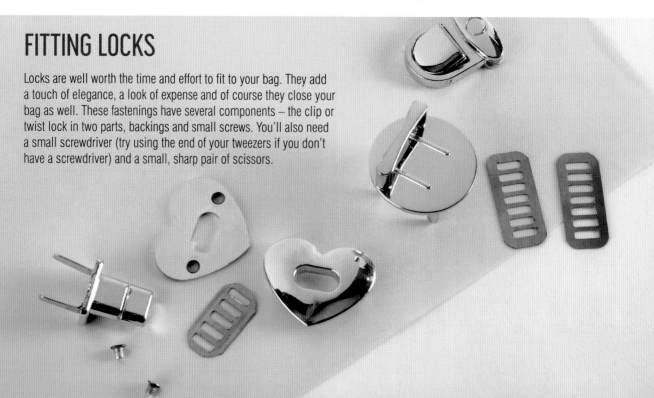

Twist lock

1 Measure and mark the required position on the flap and front of your bag. The side of the lock with the hole in it goes on the flap, the twist post is fitted to the front of the bag. Take the back of the lock, and draw around the hole and screw holes on the front of the flap.

2 Carefully cut around these markings, keeping the cut out hole small to start with; it's better to cut a hole that's too small and make it bigger than risking the hole being too big, in which case you may need to make a new flap.

3 Fit the lock to either side of the flap and screw in place.

4 Make small incisions on the front of your bag for the prongs on the back of the twist side of the lock to push through. Use the back of the lock as a template.

5 Push in the prongs, fit the backing on the inside of your bag and bend the prongs inwards.

6 This is what the finished lock should look like.

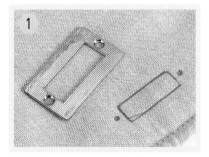
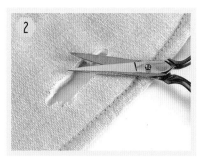
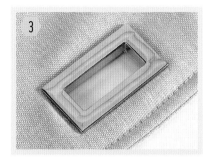

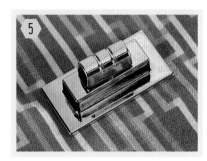
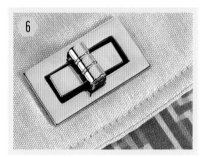
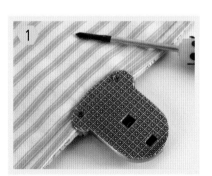
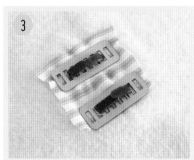

Clip lock

1 Measure and mark the position of the clip and bracket on your flap and front of your bag.

2 Make small incisions through the markings on the bag and push the prongs through.

3 Attach the back piece or pieces and bend the prongs inwards to secure.

4 The clip is fitted to the edge of the flap: it simply fits over the seam and is screwed in place. Here's a tip – if your flap is too thin it will leave a gap, so make a decorative tab from fabric and fix this to the end of the flap before fitting the snap.

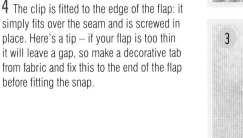

Project
TABLET CASE

78

Techniques

- Using a template
- Cutting corners and snipping curves
- Applying a magnetic snap
- Fitting a letterbox zip
- Ladder stitch

You will need

For a tablet measuring 24 × 17cm (9½ × 6¾in):
- 61 × 38cm (24 × 15in) outer fabric
- 89 × 43cm (35 × 17in) lining fabric
- 61 × 56cm (24 × 22in) wadding/batting
- Magnetic snap
- 25cm (10in) zip
- 28cm (11in) circle template
- Repositionable spray fabric adhesive

Cut

- Two pieces of outer fabric, one measuring 33 × 28cm (13 × 11in) and the other measuring 28 × 19cm (11 × 7½in)
- Four pieces of lining fabric, one measuring 33 × 28cm (13 × 11in) and three measuring 28 × 19cm (11 × 7½in)
- Two pieces of wadding/batting, one measuring 33 × 28cm (13 × 11in) and the other measuring 28 × 19cm (11 × 7½in)

1 Take the large outer and lining pieces and cut a curve from the top of each piece using your circle template. Take into account the direction of your print – fold the top of the fabric over before cutting to make sure the print won't be upside down on the flap. Fuse batting/wadding to the wrong side of the outer pieces with spray adhesive.

2 Fuse wadding/batting to the wrong side of the remaining outer piece. Apply the thicker half of the magnetic snap to the centre, 10cm (4in) from the top (see page 76).

3 Fit the second half of the snap to the centre of the curved lining piece, 2.5cm (1in) from the top.

4 Take one of the remaining lining pieces. Draw a box 20cm (8in) long on the wrong side, 4cm (1½in) from the top, to fit the zip (see page 54).

5 Fit the zip to this lining piece and the outer panel, following the instructions (you will need to trim the ends off the zip).

6 Place the remaining two lining pieces either side of the zipped panel, right sides together, and sew across the top.

7 Fold the lining pieces to the back, so that the zipped panel is at the front, and edge stitch across the top.

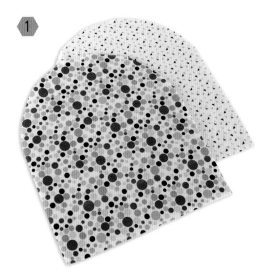

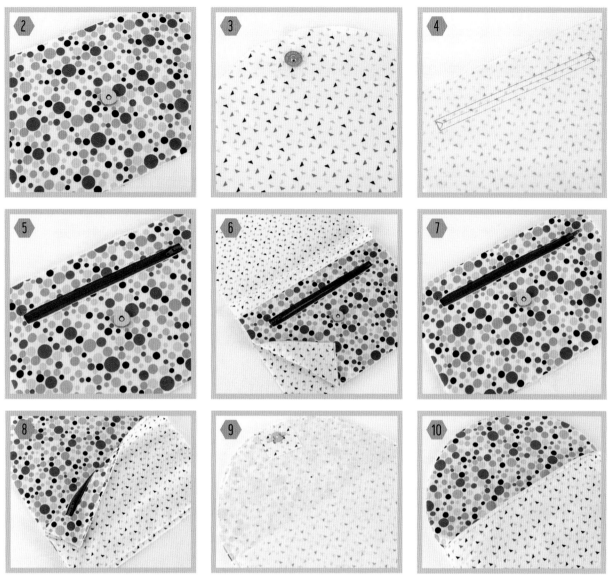

8 Place the zipped panel and the curved outer fabric piece right sides together and sew together along the bottom.

9 Place the lining piece right side down on top, sandwiching the zipped panel in the centre. Sew all the way round, leaving a turning gap of about 10cm (4in) in the bottom. Snip around the curved seam and cut off the corners.

10 Turn the right side out and sew the opening closed with a ladder stitch.

11 Turn through again and press. Edge stitch around the curved flap.

PURSE FRAMES

Choose either sew-in or glue-in metal frames. They are available in a vast range of sizes and styles.

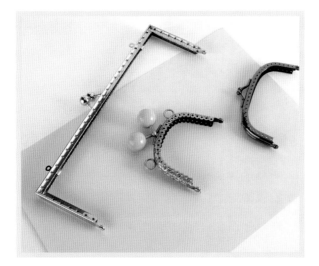

Sew-in frames.

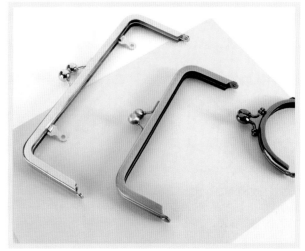

Glue-in frames.

HANDLE AND STRAPS

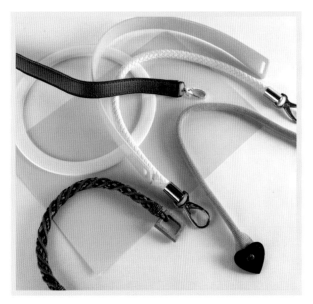

Shop-bought handles can give a bag a professional finish. Some are sewn to the outside of the bag and some will clip onto D rings.

I'm not a fan of shiny polyester webbing; I prefer the cotton-mix materials that give the webbing a matte finish. They are usually 2.5cm (1in) wide and can be cut to any length you like.

MAKING YOUR OWN FABRIC STRAPS

Make your own straps for a perfect match to your bag! Most of my bags will have a strap 2.5cm (1in) wide; I decide the length I'd like depending on the design of the bag. You can make either open-ended or closed end. The open-ended straps are sewn into the top seams of your bag, the closed ends are sewn to the front of your bag. Add interfacing or fusible fleece to the wrong side of your fabric strips if you need a stiffer handle, or a blast of spray starch can give a crisp finish.

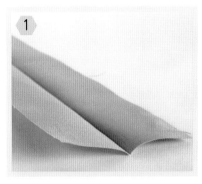

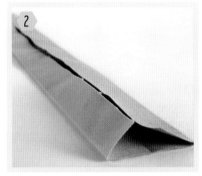

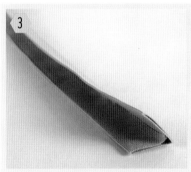

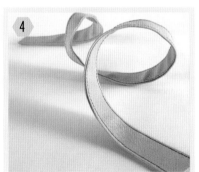

Open-ended

1 Cut out your fabric. Fold in half lengthways and press.

2 Fold the two long sides to the centre and press.

3 Fold in half again and press.

4 Top-stitch along both long sides.

Closed end

Follow steps 1–3 above.

4 Fold the long sides of the strap together so that the raw edges are on the outside. Sew across the bottom.

5 Turn the right side out and top-stitch all around the edge.

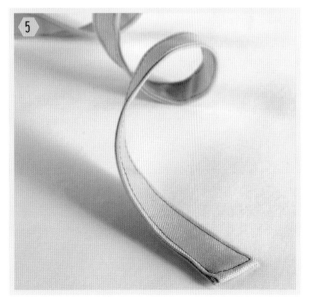

Project
FRAME PURSE

Techniques

- Making a template
- Fitting a metal frame
- Snipping into curves
- Ladder stitch

Notes

Use a 5mm (¼in) seam allowance

You will need

- Paper and pen
- Metal purse frame (any size or shape you like), plus wet glue if you're using a glue-in frame
- Outer fabric, wadding/batting and lining, the size depends on the size of purse you're making – measure your finished template and cut your fabric accordingly
- Strong thread – I've used six strands of embroidery thread
- Large-eyed needle
- Erasable marker pen

1 Take a piece of paper and draw around the outside of the purse frame from one hinge to the other.

2 Swing the hinge to one side by 2.5cm (1in). Draw a line here.

3 The belly of the bag can be any size and shape you like: round or square. Draw a few options and choose which one you're happiest with. Fold the pattern in half before cutting out, this will make sure it is symmetrical.

4 Cut two outer and two lining pieces of fabric from your pattern. (On fine fabric, you may need to add wadding or fusible fleece to the wrong side.)

5 Place the hinge over the lining pieces and make a mark at the base of the hinge. Make sure the marks are in the same position on each piece. Sew each lining piece right sides together to an outer piece, around the top, from one mark to another.

6 Sew the bottom of the two outer pieces right sides together, then repeat with the lining pieces to and from the same markings. This time leave a turning gap in the base. Clip into any curved seams in the base of the purse pieces, but avoid clipping into the top that fits inside the purse frame. The extra bulk is helpful to hold the fabric inside the frame.

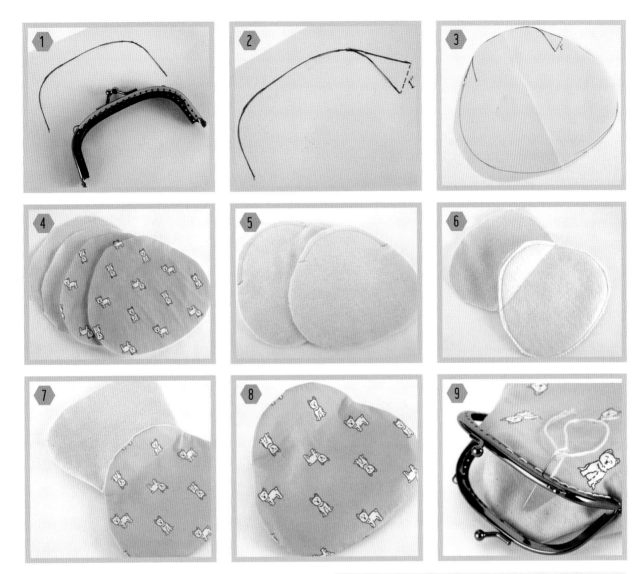

7 Turn the right side out, sew up the turning gap.

8 Press, then push the lining inside the purse.

9 Fold the top of each side of the purse in half and mark the centre point. For a sew-in frame, push a needle and knotted thread through this point, then take the needle through the middle hole of one side of the frame. This way you can ensure the purse will sit centrally in the frame. Sew through every other hole, picking up the edge of the purse as you sew. When you reach the hinge, go back through the holes to create a 'backstitch' effect. Repeat across the second side of the frame, then on the opposite side. If you have trouble tying off the thread neatly, cut the thread to about 12mm (½in) in length, tuck it inside the frame and add a spot of wet glue to secure.

Tip

For a glue-in frame, drizzle a little strong, wet glue into one side of the frame. Leave it for a minute or so to set slightly then, using tweezers, carefully push the fabric into the frame, starting in the centre. You should have a bit of 'wiggle time' before the glue dries. Leave one side to dry completely before moving onto the second side.

Project
TOTE BAG

Techniques

- Making bag handles
- Using a circle template
- Bias binding
- Making a square bag base
- Adding a magnetic snap
- Decorative seams

Notes

Use a 5mm (¼in) seam allowance

You will need

- 71 × 30cm (28 × 12in) patterned fabric
- 35.5 × 18cm (14 × 7in) contrasting fabric
- 76 × 71cm (30 × 28in) lining fabric
- 71 × 63.5cm (28 × 25in) fusible fleece
- Magnetic snap
- 7.5cm (3in) circle template
- Repositionable fabric glue stick
- Erasable marker pen

Cut

- Two pieces of patterned fabric measuring 35.5 × 30cm (14 × 12in)
- Two pieces of contrasting fabric measuring 35.5 × 9cm (14 × 3½in)
- Two pieces of lining fabric measuring 41 × 35.5cm (16¼ × 14in)
- Two pieces of fusible fleece measuring 39 × 35.5cm (15¼ × 14in)
- Two pieces of lining fabric for the handles measuring 51 × 10cm (20 × 4in)
- Two pieces of fusible fleece for the handles measuring 51 × 10cm (20 × 4in)
- Two pieces of lining fabric for the decorative panel measuring 38 × 5cm (15 × 2in)
- Four pieces of lining fabric for the fastening measuring 7.5 × 7.5cm (3 × 3in)

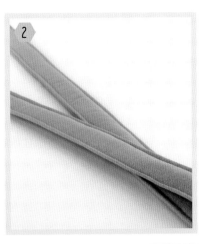

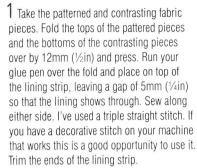

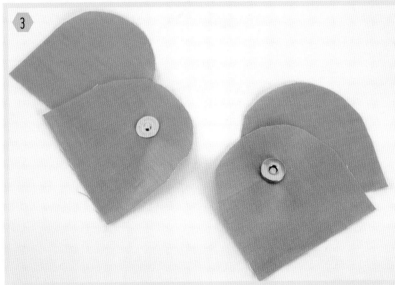

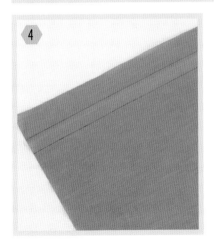

1 Take the patterned and contrasting fabric pieces. Fold the tops of the pattered pieces and the bottoms of the contrasting pieces over by 12mm (½in) and press. Run your glue pen over the fold and place on top of the lining strip, leaving a gap of 5mm (¼in) so that the lining shows through. Sew along either side. I've used a triple straight stitch. If you have a decorative stitch on your machine that works this is a good opportunity to use it. Trim the ends of the lining strip.

2 Fuse fleece to the wrong sides of these panels, and to the wrong sides of the handle pieces. Make up two open-ended straps for the handles as on page 81.

3 Use your circle template to curve one end of the 7.5cm (3in) square fastening pieces. Apply the magnetic snap to two pieces, centrally, 2.5cm (1in) from the curved end (see page 76).

4 Sew each snap piece right sides together to a plain piece leaving the straight side open. Turn the right side out and press, then edge stitch around the seam. Take the two lining pieces and draw two lines on the wrong side with an erasable marker, 4cm (1½in) and 6.5cm (2½in) from the top. Fold the two lines together and crease along the centre.

5 Mark the centre point of this crease, then place the tabs inside the crease, one with the snap facing up, and the other with the snap facing down. Fold over the fabric and sew along your drawn lines.

6 Open out and press. Tack/baste the handles, facing downwards, to the top of the outer pieces, 12.5cm (5in) from either side. Make sure the handles are not twisted.

7 Cut a 4cm (1½in) square from the bottom corners of each outer and lining piece.

8 Sew the tops of the lining pieces right sides together to the tops of the outer pieces.

Here you have a simple, useful tote.

9 Place the two sections right sides together, sew all the way round starting at the side seams to make sure they match. Remember, nobody notices a perfectly matching seam, but they'll notice a bad one. Leave a turning gap in the base of the lining of about 10cm (4in), and don't sew the cut-out corners. Pinch the corners and sew to make the base square (see pages 72–73). Turn the right side out and sew the opening closed.

10 Push the lining inside the bag and press. Edge stitch around the top.

PLEATING AND PIN TUCKS

A pleated frill around a pillow cover creates a crisp, modern trim. The key is to fold even pleats across strips of folded fabric. This may be time-consuming, but worth the effort. You'll need to measure around your pillow cover, then multiply the length of trim fabric by three. Pleats also work well around the hem of aprons or little girls' dresses!

Pin tucks look smart on a man's dress shirt, but also add texture to your project by raising the fabric in between the rows of stitches slightly. Use the technique on bags to create an expensive, quilted look, either by sewing a few rows as a border, or cross-hatching (sewing in a grid-like manner) across your fabric.

PLEATING

Here are two different pleating techniques you can try:

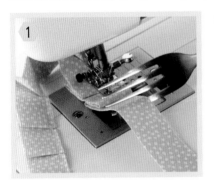

1 Place the raw edge of a piece of fabric under your sewing machine needle. Take the fabric over the bottom prong of your fork.

2 Fold the fork over twice to form a pleat. Carefully remove the fork, sew over the pleat and repeat all the way around the fabric hoops.

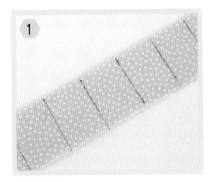

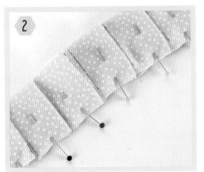

1 Alternatively, fold your fabric in half lengthways, measure and mark 2.5cm (1in) intervals with an erasable marker.

2 Pinch the marks on the fabric strip and fold them together, pin, then sew, removing the pins as you go.

PIN TUCKS

With your twin needle in your sewing machine, and increased tension, sew rows of lines across the fabric to create pin tucks (see page 21). A pin tuck foot will help to keep your stitching in even lines. As with the needles, they are available in different widths.

Project
BOLSTER PILLOW

Techniques

⊕ Pleating
⊕ Pin tucks

Notes

Use a 5mm (¼in) seam allowance

You will need

⊕ Bolster pillow pad. Mine is 41cm (16in) long, 15cm (6in) across the round end and 48cm (19in) circumference
⊕ 84×61cm (33×24in) fabric – I've used a quilting cotton (a heavier weight of fabric won't gather as tightly at the ends of the bolster)
⊕ 152×20cm (60×8in) contrasting fabric for the pleats
⊕ 51cm (20in) of ribbon, 5mm (¼in) wide, to gather
⊕ 102cm (40in) of ribbon, 12mm (½in) wide, to decorate
⊕ 102cm (40in) of lace, 5mm (¼in) wide
⊕ Twin needle for your sewing machine
⊕ Fork
⊕ Safety pin

1 Cut a piece of fabric measuring 53×46cm (21×18in). Sew pin tucks across the fabric, 4cm (1½in) apart (see page 21). Trim the fabric to measure 51×43cm (20×17in). The fabric is cut larger at the beginning to allow for shrinkage from the stitching. Sew the two long ends right sides together to form a tube. Cut the contrasting fabric into two lengths, each measuring 152×10cm (60×4in). Sew the short ends right sides together to make two hoops, then press in half lengthways, wrong sides together. Make pleats as shown on page 87. Thread one pleated loop over each end of the right side of the fabric tube, raw edges together, and sew.

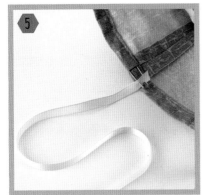

2 Cut two lengths of fabric each measuring 51 × 11cm (20 × 4¼in). Sew the two short ends right sides together to make two tubes. Press the seam open, then fold the top over by 12mm (½in), twice, and hem. Thread these tubes over the pleated fabric, right sides together and matching up the seams. Sew around the raw edges.

3 Open out and press.

4 When the end of the cover is gathered, there may be a small gap in the centre. So that you don't see the pillow pad through this hole, tack a 10cm (4in) circle of fabric to each end of the pad.

5 Push the pillow pad into the cover. Cut in half the ribbon that is 5mm (¼in) wide. Unpick a few stitches in the seam of the hem, thread one end of the ribbon onto your safety pin and thread through the channel.

6 Pull the ribbon to gather tightly, then knot. Trim off the ends of the ribbon and tuck the knot inside. Repeat for the opposite end of the pillow.

7 Cut the remaining ribbon and lace in half and tie together to make two bows. Hand stitch to each end of the bolster.

QUILTING

My first attempt at patchwork was in a class some twenty years ago. This led to my first project, a hand-sewn cover for a stool, using shades of denim in a 'tumbling blocks' design. Thank goodness for thimbles!

Patchwork and quilting are two different sewing techniques that can come together to make a 'quilt'. Patchwork is a method of sewing together pieces of fabric to form a pattern, quilting is the technique used to sew together multiple layers of fabric and wadding. Therefore, a patchworked piece of work doesn't necessarily have to be quilted, and you can quilt over a plain piece of fabric!

WHERE TO START

Purchase a self-healing cutting board, ruler and rotary cutter – these often come as a pack and can ensure precise cutting. Acrylic rulers and templates for quilting are available in many shapes and sizes; some will have the seam allowances marked and are transparent, to enable you to 'fussy cut' your fabric (see page 48).

CHOOSE PRE-CUTS

Simple shapes are easier for a beginner to sew – stick to squares and rectangles at first. Try pre-cut fabrics (see page 30) in squares or strips, or a mixture of both!

SEAM ALLOWANCE

Sewing an accurate 5mm (¼in) seam allowance is essential. If your machine doesn't come with a 5mm (¼in) foot, it's worth considering purchasing one; otherwise move your needle into a position which will give you 5mm (¼in) from the edge of your existing machine foot.

FABRIC, WADDING/BATTING AND THREAD

Use good quality 100 per cent cotton fabric for general piecing and appliqué. Buy the best you can afford. If your fabric is finer, consider using spray starch, which will help with both the cutting and sewing. With cotton fabric, use a 100 per cent cotton thread (50wt) for both machine and hand piecing (see page 35). When it comes to wadding the choice is vast, but a wool/polyester mix is a good option for a bed quilt and works well with both hand and machine quilting. I'd suggest pre-washing your fabric to prevent your quilt from shrinking (although some quilters prefer this as it gives a vintage look). Read the manufacturer's instructions for your wadding – it should inform you of the expected shrinkage, if any.

PRESSING SEAMS

Some quilters choose to press the seams to one side, some prefer to press open. Pressing a seam open can help the seam to lie flat but will weaken it; pressing to the side is advisable if one fabric is paler than the other so that the dark fabric doesn't show through.

LAYERING

You will have backing fabric, top fabric and wadding in the middle. Cut your backing fabric and wadding slightly larger than needed to allow for movement. Press your backing fabric and lay it flat. Place the wadding on top and smooth it over to make it flat. The quilt top sits over these two layers. Starting in the centre, either pin with quilting pins (slightly bent safety pins) or sew tacking/basting stitches every 10–15cm (4–6in). Alternatively, use fabric spray adhesive to sandwich your three quilt layers together for speed.

MATERIALS

If you're machine quilting, use a slightly finer thread (40wt) and invest in a walking foot (this enables the three layers of material to feed evenly through the machine). If you're free-motion machine quilting, you'll need a darning foot and don't forget to lower or cover your feed dogs. A lighter weight cotton thread to match your underside fabric would work well in your machine bobbin. If you're hand quilting, use fairly short lengths of hand-quilting thread and run these through a beeswax block to deter knotting. Use a hand-quilting needle (these are very fine with a small eye and will test your eyesight!). I recommend using a thimble on your finger. I prefer leather thimbles to prevent the needle from slipping. Now sew through all layers of your quilt sandwich to create the pattern you require – this could be a specific design, squiggly or straight lines. Quilt frames are available which help to keep large quilts flat as you sew.

STITCHING IN THE DITCH

This method is simply sewing into an existing seam. A special foot is available for your sewing machine with a guide in the centre to help with accurate stitching.

BINDING

Traditionally, single-fold bias binding is used for quilts as it is more durable than double fold, but it is applied in the same way (see the section on bias binding on page 66).

FIND A FRIEND

Finally, new quilters should consider taking a class, either locally or online. Start your quilting journey in a small way: make some blocks which can later be joined together – three or four will make a table runner or wall hanging – then progress onto a larger project. Join a group or online forum where you'll pick up lots of information, tips and help. You'll soon want to progress onto other skills and techniques but be warned, once you've got the quilting bug, you'll never stop!

Project
MACHINE MAT

Techniques

- Bias binding
- Quilting
- Slip stitch

Notes

Use a 5mm (¼in) seam allowance
I'd suggest cutting the fabrics larger than needed initially, in case the layers move as you quilt

You will need

- 91.5 × 41cm (36 × 16in) main cotton fabric
- 91.5 × 41cm (36 × 16in) wadding/batting
- 91.5 × 41cm (36 × 16in) contrasting cotton fabric, for the base
- 203cm (80in) of bias binding, 2cm (¾in) wide
- Erasable marker pen
- Ruler
- Repositionable spray fabric adhesive

1 Spray the wrong sides of the two fabric pieces and place either side of the wadding/batting. Take your ruler and marking pen and draw a 4cm (1½in) grid over the outer fabric.

2 Sew a straight stitch over each line. If you have a walking foot it will help to feed the layers of fabric through the machine easily. Remove the drawn lines, then trim the rectangle to 86 × 35.5cm (34 × 14in).

3 Machine sew a strip of bias binding to the back of the right-hand short end (see page 67).

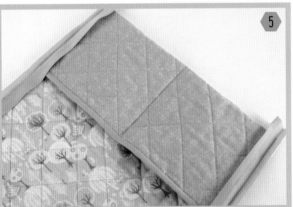

4 Fold the tape over the edge of the fabric and hand sew with a slip stitch. Fold the end of the strip over by 12.5cm (5in) to form the pockets. Sew along each side within the seam allowance, then measure the centre of the pocket, mark, then sew to divide into two. (You can, of course, make as many pockets as you like – a few slim pockets for pens could be useful…)

5 Machine sew the bias tape around the three raw edges, extending the ends of the tape by 12mm (½in). Mitre the corners as you sew.

6 Wrap the ends of the tape neatly around the fabric, then hand sew all the way around with a slip stitch.

DRESSMAKING

Dressmaking is where it all started for me, albeit making clothes for my dolls and teddies! My first venture into fashion was in the early 1970s... remember hot pants?

If you want to dip your toes into the world of dressmaking, here are a few basic tips. I would advise going to a class to learn in-depth techniques such as pattern adjustments; these are worthwhile skills to learn as it's rare to find a pattern that will fit you perfectly without a few tweaks.

PATTERNS

⊕ As a beginner sewer, the most obvious advice is to buy a simple pattern. Many patterns will include a skill level on the packaging. Don't be overambitious with collars, cuffs, pockets and linings. Your skills will quickly grow with practice and you'll be incorporating these things soon enough.

⊕ Study the pattern packaging before buying fabric. There is a lot of essential information on there, including what type of fabric and how much to buy, any notions needed (zips, hooks and eyes, buttons etc), and most importantly, measurements.

⊕ Don't buy a pattern for your shop-bought dress size, go by your body measurements, as there may be a substantial difference in sizing.

⊕ If you're choosing a pattern from a catalogue, take a look at the back of the book where you'll find vital information on measuring and fitting.

INTERFACING

You'll use interfacing to support areas like necklines. It comes in many different weights, either fusible (iron-on) or sew-in. Take advice from your pattern instructions and/or your fabric supplier.

CHOOSING FABRIC

If you're a beginner, choose fabric with a small all-over pattern. Avoid one-way designs, large patterns or fabric with a nap (textured fabric which lies one way, e.g. velvet). Plain fabrics will tend to show any signs of a wobbly stitch or pucker, and patterns that need matching will require extra fabric. If you're buying fabric from a shop, ask the advice of the assistant if you're uncertain.

CHOOSING THREADS

Choose a thread appropriate to your fabric type and weight: cotton thread for cotton fabric, polyester thread for man-made fabrics.

MAKING A START

⊕ Find a large, flat surface, with plenty of room, to spread everything out on.

⊕ Study your pattern and read through all the instructions first. These will advise the most economical way to lay out your fabric, which pattern pieces to cut and which way to place the pattern pieces over your fabric.

⊕ Choose the pattern pieces required for your garment and dry-iron the tissue flat. If there are any creases in your pattern it will affect the size of your fabric piece.

⊕ If using a multi-size pattern, you might find it easier to highlight on the pattern around the size you are making. It's also useful to highlight the number of each pattern piece to cut. Cut out the pattern pieces in the size you require.

⊕ If lengthening or shortening a pattern, use the guidelines on the pattern pieces. Don't adjust from the hemline unless advised.

⊕ Pin the pattern pieces to your fabric, then take your time cutting out the shapes. Pattern pieces fit together like a jigsaw so it's vital to cut accurately! It's always advisable to make up a 'toille' (a practice piece) in cheaper fabric first, then you can make any adjustments needed before committing to your chosen fabric.

⊕ To pre-wash or not is an ongoing debate. I always pre-wash fabric for dressmaking, just in case there is any shrinkage.

⊕ Ensure you transfer all notches, dots and markings onto your material; these are important for matching up your pattern pieces, and when adding darts and zips.

JARGON-BUSTER

Seams and hems are explained in other chapters in this book (see pages 46–47 and 49), but here are some of the more routine sewing mysteries explained:

Darts

These give shape to your garment. Reproduce markings on both sides of the fabric and sew. To get a sharp point to the inner end of the dart, knot thread ends together to secure, rather than using reverse stitch.

Graduated seam allowance

If using thick fabric, cut your seam allowance to differing widths, to lessen bulk in the seams.

Pressing

'Pressing' means placing the iron over the seams without pushing it. This helps to set the seams without distorting the fabric. Using a steam press, ensure you press after every instruction.

Stay stitching

This is usually around necklines and curves where fabric is likely to stretch. Sew 12mm (½in) from the edge of the fabric as indicated on the pattern.

Under-stitching

This helps facings to stay on the inside and not be seen. Fold the seam allowance towards the facing and sew through both the facing and seam allowance, as close to the seam line as you can.

Ease stitching

Increase the straight stitch size on your machine and run a long stitch along the seam allowance between the two points indicated on your pattern, leaving the threads long. Gather the fabric by gently pulling on the bobbin thread, sliding the fabric to tighten without gathering. This technique is usually used when fitting curved pieces such as the top of sleeves.

Hopefully, these tips will help you to successfully create a garment you are proud to wear!

INDEX